Praise for *Is Justice Possible?*

Justice is fleeting, yet demanded. It's essential, yet often missed. We live in a broken world in need of just solutions—and Paul Nyquist brings a biblical focus and discerning look at why justice matters and how we might work toward it.

ED STETZER
Billy Graham Chair, Wheaton College

Paul Nyquist has given us a path to justice. Christians know the One from whom justice is derived, he writes, and we must be on the front lines wherever there is injustice. Injustice is a natural occurrence in a fallen world and Nyquist calls for Christians to take seriously the injustice in the American judicial system and to help mend its disturbing impact at all levels. *Is Justice Possible?* is a meaningful book for groups, filled with biblical study as well as practical and proactive steps to get involved.

WILLIAM E. BROWN
Senior Fellow for Worldview and Culture, The Colson Center for Christian Worldview

This book tackles the controversial topic of justice, so often discussed today. Nyquist helps us understand why justice often eludes us in this life, but also how we must work to achieve it as best we can. It helped me understand the issues at stake and renewed my vision to work for justice at every level. Thankfully it ended with a discussion of God the judge who will, in the end, bring perfect justice to a broken world.

ERWIN W. LUTZER
Pastor Emeritus, The Moody Church, Chicago

Christians who take the Bible seriously dare not ignore this message. Paul Nyquist writes like an Old Testament prophet in modern America . . . confronting injustice and calling us to step up and do what is right.

LEITH ANDERSON
President, National Association of Evangelicals, Washington, D.C.

Unfortunately, justice is elusive in this fallen world. Yet, as followers of Jesus, we are called to do the right thing—confronting injustice, serving the poor, and defending the dignity of the incarcerated. In *Is Justice Possible?*, Paul Nyquist challenges us with stories, biblical truth, and passion to go beyond our comfort zone to relentlessly pursue justice. May this book spawn a new army of believers committed to this cause, which is dear to the heart of our God.

JAMES J. ACKERMAN
President & Chief Executive Officer, Prison Fellowship

Is justice possible? That is a question this book asks by taking a careful and serious look at justice in Scripture and in our own history. Justice is a key value in Scripture that we often sidestep. Nyquist's study shows that. He also shows how we can do better and where the best hope for justice lies. The book is full of insight. In sum, justice is well served by this book.

DARRELL BOCK
Executive Director for Cultural Engagement, Howard G. Hendricks Center for Christian Leadership and Cultural Engagement; Senior Research Professor of New Testament Studies, Dallas Theological Seminary

Is Justice Possible? is a watershed work for evangelicals committed to the quest for the justice of Christ in the legal systems of man. Nyquist captures the ethos and heartache of those crying out, "How long, oh Lord, until justice comes?" Through the use of theology, history, and practical legal skill, Nyquist takes us on a journey that, though at times painful, ultimately lands in the hope of the gospel. This is a must read for those who are confident that in Christ we have a promise of divine justice and who long to see this promise more clearly in our fallen world!

CHRIS BROOKS
Campus Dean, Moody Theological Seminary – Michigan

We live in a fallen world, which is cluttered with evil deeds—stealing, brutality, murder. However, God calls us all to be just in dealing with people who are accused of violating the law. But is justice possible—especially since we've all sinned and fallen short of God's standard of righteousness? Paul Nyquist has addressed this question nobly from a biblical point of view. It's an honest evaluation of where we, as a nation, have fallen short, and what we should be doing about it—realizing that someday Christ will reign as the perfect judge!

GENE A. GETZ
Professor, pastor, author

IS
JUSTICE
POSSIBLE?

THE ELUSIVE PURSUIT
OF WHAT IS RIGHT

J. PAUL NYQUIST

MOODY PUBLISHERS

CHICAGO

Scripture quotations are from the ESV® Bible (The Holy Bible, English Standard Version®), copyright © 2001 by Crossway, a publishing ministry of Good News Publishers. Used by permission. All rights reserved.

Italics used in quotations are those of the author.

Edited by Matthew Boffey
Interior and Cover Design: Erik Peterson
Cover image of marker strokes copyright (c) 2016 by swatchandsoda/Shutterstock (63596539). All rights reserved.
Author photo: Cynthia Howe

All websites listed herein are accurate at the time of publication but may change in the future or cease to exist. The listing of website references and resources does not imply publisher endorsement of the site's entire contents. Groups and organizations are listed for informational purposes, and listing does not imply publisher endorsement of their activities.

Library of Congress Cataloging-in-Publication Data

Names: Nyquist, J. Paul, author.
Title: Is justice possible? : the elusive pursuit of what is right / J. Paul
  Nyquist.
Description: Chicago : Moody Publishers, 2017. | Includes bibliographical
  references.
Identifiers: LCCN 2016045871 (print) | LCCN 2016049377 (ebook) | ISBN
  9780802414946 | ISBN 9780802495105
Subjects: LCSH: Christianity and justice. | Justice.
Classification: LCC BR115.J8 N97 2017 (print) | LCC BR115.J8 (ebook) | DDC
  241/.622--dc23
LC record available at https://lccn.loc.gov/2016045871

We hope you enjoy this book from Moody Publishers. Our goal is to provide high-quality, thought-provoking books and products that connect truth to your real needs and challenges. For more information on other books and products written and produced from a biblical perspective, go to www.moodypublishers.com or write to:

Moody Publishers
820 N. LaSalle Boulevard
Chicago, IL 60610

1 3 5 7 9 10 8 6 4 2

Printed in the United States of America

To Cheryl

"Behold, you are beautiful, my love;
Behold, you are beautiful."
—Song of Solomon 1:15

CONTENTS

INTRODUCTION

For I, the LORD, love justice.
—ISAIAH 61:8

D ana Holland woke abruptly at 6:00 a.m. on February 22, 1993, when his uncle returned to the apartment they shared at 7821 South Paulina on Chicago's South Side. Rubbing sleep from his eyes, Holland climbed out of bed. When he took out the trash, police spotted him and took him into custody. At that moment, Holland's nightmare began.

Prosecutors first charged him with raping a twenty-two-year-old woman. The crime had occurred earlier that morning in an alley near Holland's apartment. While he was in custody, Holland was also charged with the robbery and attempted murder of Ella Wembley, which had occurred nearby two weeks prior.

Two years later, in February of 1995, Holland stood trial in the Cook County Circuit Court for the robbery and attempted murder charges. Although prosecutors produced just one witness and circumstantial evidence, Holland was convicted and sentenced to twenty-eight years in prison.

The rape trial took place in April of 1997. The judge denied an attempt to obtain DNA testing on seminal evidence. Testimony in defense of Holland from his uncle, Gordon Bolden, was roundly dismissed by the Illinois State Attorney's office. Holland was ultimately convicted of three counts of aggravated criminal sexual assault and sentenced by Circuit Court Judge Themis N. Kamezis to thirty years in prison for each count. Furthermore, the judge ruled that the sentences be served consecutively. Dana Holland faced 118 years in prison—far longer than he could expect to live.[1]

But he was innocent. Holland's long road to exoneration began when law students connected with Northwestern University's School of Law accepted his case in 2002. DNA testing proved the perpetrator in the rape case was not Holland, but his uncle. Accordingly, the judge vacated the conviction. New evidence was introduced at a 2003 retrial of the Wembley crime, and Holland was acquitted.

He walked free on June 6, 2003. He had spent 3,756 nights in prison and missed a decade of life with his wife and young son. All for something he did not do.

I wish I could say Dana Holland was alone in his wrongful conviction. But many others have shared his traumatic experience. Coincidentally, Holland's cellmate at the maximum security prison in Menard, Illinois—Christopher Coleman—was also wrongly convicted. Coleman was convicted of home invasion and related crimes in 1994. The judge sentenced him to two consecutive thirty-year prison terms—sixty years—but Coleman was also innocent.

With Holland's help, the student legal team at Northwestern University accepted Coleman's case. New, compelling evidence was introduced, and in 2013 the Illinois Supreme Court reversed the convictions. Coleman was released on November 26, 2013, just in time to enjoy his first Thanksgiving with his family in nineteen years.

A HUMAN PROBLEM

When I read stories like those of Dana Holland and Christopher Coleman, I feel an intense, physical reaction. My stomach tightens. My breathing slows. My head shakes. I experience a profound yearning for justice. And, like you, I grieve when I learn of yet another case of injustice. R. C. Sproul expresses this well when he writes, "Few things grieve the human soul more bitterly than the taste of injustice. It is one thing to feel the lash of the whip when we are guilty; but to be victims of punishment when we are innocent is exceedingly difficult to bear."[2]

We are wired this way by our God. We crave justice. We want what is right. We mourn the miscarriage of justice. We loathe what is wrong. This is a human thing.

Yet, as we are painfully aware, far too often our human society falls short of justice. We sometimes don't get it right. The innocent—like Holland and Coleman—are convicted and punished. The guilty escape accountability. Systems designed to bring justice fail, and we find ourselves lamenting, "Justice is far from us, and righteousness does not overtake us . . . we walk in gloom. We grope for the wall like the blind; we grope like those who have no eyes; we stumble at noon as in the twilight, among those in full vigor we are like dead men. . . . we hope for justice, but there is none" (Isa. 59:9–11).

In our grieving and groping, we would like to conveniently blame a legal system for shortchanged justice. But we cannot. This is not a legal problem; this is a human problem. We try to get it right—and often do—but sometimes we don't. Sometimes, even with the best of intentions, investigation, and deliberation, we get it wrong. And when we get it wrong, we point fingers. We blame systems. We protest. We grieve. But we fail to see the critical reality of how justice falls victim to the human factor.

While administrated by man, justice is not rooted in man. Justice is ultimately rooted in God and His righteousness. Therefore, establishing right expectations for justice in this world requires not a crash course in our legal system but a deep dive into the biblical and theological underpinnings of justice.

TWO KINDS OF JUSTICE

Two kinds of justice exist in our world, and they interact with each other.

1. Justice we see in the streets: the way we treat each other in daily interactions, how we relate to each other. Are we fair? Are we honest? Are we equitable? This is often called *social justice*. This is the justice that is violated when the vulnerable of society are abused or mistreated by the more powerful or privileged.

Social justice was a particular target of the Old Testament prophets, who railed against wrongs suffered by the widows, orphans, and strangers. In Isaiah 10:1–2 we read, "Woe to those who decree iniquitous decrees, and the writers who keep writing oppression, to turn aside the needy from justice and to rob the poor of my people of their right, that widows may be their spoil, and that they may make the fatherless their prey!" Social justice— or the lack thereof—is the justice we see in the streets.

2. Justice we see in the courts: legal justice rendered by a judge or ruling authority. While people can wrongly seek to take matters into their own hands (as through a lynch mob), legal justice is properly executed by designated authorities. This is sometimes called *corrective justice*. In biblical times, judges would sit at the gates of the city and render judgments between those engaged in a dispute. In rare occasions even a king like Solomon could act as a judge, like when he settled a dispute between two women claiming the same child (1 Kings 3:16–28). This is the kind of justice we see in the courts.

Though distinct, these two kinds of justice are related. If I violate social norms (social justice) and treat others wrongly, I may face a penalty (corrective justice), if those norms have been codified into laws. But if I comply with social norms and treat others fairly, I can expect to escape penalty. Typically the violation of one type of justice leads to the enforcement of the other type.

For example, if I rob a blind man holding a white cane as he carefully navigates a sidewalk, I can anticipate legal judgment; I've broken the social norms of the land. But if I choose to assist an elderly lady with her walker across the treacherous streets of Chicago, I can be confident of incurring no such judgment; my actions affirm the values and norms of the land.

We expect these results. But when we experience something different—or even opposite—we suffer *injustice*. This was the experience of Dana Holland and Christopher Coleman. They were innocent of the crimes that incarcerated them but were severely punished by society. In addition, those who committed wrong escaped their due punishments. This too is injustice.

This book will only focus on the justice we see in the courts: legal justice. Social justice issues certainly abound in our world, but good minds have already addressed them in penetrating works from a biblical perspective.[3] I would only add clutter to their reasoned and passionate arguments, if I attempted to speak on both social and legal justice.

In comparison to social justice, legal justice has been fairly neglected. As a result, we as Christians often have unrealistic expectations of our legal system. We expect the perfect administration of justice through our courts. We are disappointed when stories like that of Dana Holland and Christopher Coleman emerge. Yet as I already stated, the problem is not legal; it is disturbingly human. True corrective justice in this present world will always remain elusive.

Right now you may be wondering, "What's it to me? I'm not a lawyer or a judge, so what can I do about the shortcomings in our legal system, even if they are reflections of a human problem?" That's a fair question. For most of us, concerns of legal justice are far off our radars. We pay our taxes, obey the laws (except for occasionally speeding), and begrudgingly respond to jury duty. Most of our concerns revolve around our own lives: securing a good job, finding a godly spouse, raising children who love the Lord, growing in our faith, etc.—good things, to be sure. But God calls us to more. He calls us to care for our neighbors and the outsiders. Jesus commands each of us, "Love your neighbor as yourself" (Matt. 19:19).

Our neighbor is not just the friend we bump into at Walmart or the barista we know at the corner coffee shop. Increasingly in this country our neighbor is the one incarcerated in our jails and prisons. Like floodwaters pouring over the banks of a river, our penal system is overflowing with inmates from a broken judicial system—many of whom rightly belong in prison—and some who don't. Admittedly, I am no legal expert, but as a minister of the gospel and a follower of Jesus, I am under compulsion to speak. This critical issue has been weighing on my heart for some time, and with the help of a researcher and other counsel, I have sought to lift the curtain on legal injustice in the United States and outline a Christian response.

STRUCTURE OF THE BOOK

To explore this vital subject, this book is organized into four sections, each addressing a key question.

In Part One I answer the question, "What is justice?" This may seem unnecessary to ponder, but like the foundation of a building, this basic question is where we must start. Everyone has their own ideas of what constitutes justice, and these ideas may contradict each other. How can what's right to one person not be right to another? How can justice mean different things to different people? I will show how justice has its starting point in God, not in man. We will study Scripture together to see how the biblical terms of *righteousness*, *justice*, and *holiness* all contribute to an accurate understanding of what is right.

Part Two asks the perennial question, "Why is justice elusive?" It can feel as difficult to grasp as a soap bubble dancing in the breeze. I will give four reasons why we yearn for justice yet often fail to attain it. These reasons are inherently linked to mankind and our depravity, and this reality must temper our expectations for justice. While we have a legal system, we do not necessarily have a justice system.

While we have a legal system, we do not necessarily have a justice system.

In Part Three I address the question, "How should we do justice?" If justice is elusive, what does God expect of us as His children? I will move from the theological to the practical and show what justice means for us in the political, public, and personal arenas. While we may be imperfect in the application of justice because of our fallen humanity, this does not relieve us of our duty before God to pursue justice.

Finally, in Part Four I discuss the question, "Will we ever see justice in this world?" We yearn for it. We long to see justice administered consistently and fairly for all. Yet the drag of our depravity is an unwanted yoke skewing our judgment. We must admit that, despite our best efforts, true justice will never be fully realized in this age. More injustice, like that experienced by Dana Holland and Christopher Coleman, will unfortunately occur, and we need to correctly calibrate our expectations.

In spite of this there is hope: a different day is coming. God gives us the encouraging and comforting promise that one day, when the just King rules this world, justice will be perfectly and consistently enforced on the earth. While we wait for that day, we bear the responsibility and privilege to pursue justice to the best of our ability—in our community, nation, and world. I hope that this book's theological framework and practical ideas will assist you in this calling.

PART ONE

WHAT IS JUSTICE?

CHAPTER 1

THE STARTING POINT FOR JUSTICE

When the latest Star Wars movie released over the 2015 Christmas holidays, I went to see it at the local theater with several members of my family. Since I live in urban, downtown Chicago, we walked to a theater near Michigan Avenue. After the movie, as we were stepping back outside, I heard loud voices. I followed the sound and almost ran into a crowd of approximately two hundred people—surrounded by nearly as many police officers—marching down the center of Michigan Avenue.

"Sixteen shots! Sixteen shots!" they chanted. I knew immediately what the protest was about. Chicago had recently erupted over the release of a video from October 2014 that showed a police officer killing an unarmed, African American teenager— Laquan MacDonald—by shooting him sixteen times. The marching crowd was peaceful but focused. As they pressed down the street, they held signs demanding, *We Want Justice!*

But what is justice?

If I had polled the protestors and asked them what justice they desired, I would have received many different answers. Some would want a lengthy prison term for the guilty police officer.

Some would want capital punishment. Some would want to overthrow the Chicago power structure.

The protestors marched together. They cried out in unison. But their demands for justice would mean many different outcomes.

THE WRONG STARTING POINT

How can ten different people come to ten different answers on what is just in a situation?

Why is there not complete agreement?

They have the wrong starting point. Even from the days of the ancient Greek philosophers (like Aristotle, Plato, and Socrates), the starting point of justice has been man. Definitions of justice abounded among the ancients, but they inevitably included ideas of fairness, equality, honesty, and equity. For example, Aristotle said, "Justice consists in what is lawful and fair, with fairness involving equitable distributions and the correction of what is inequitable."[1]

> **How can ten different people come to ten different answers on what is just in a situation?**

Through the centuries philosophers have debated the same themes, creating their own flavors of justice. John Locke argued that justice started with the protection of people's natural rights.[2] But who determines this list of rights? What if states—or countries—disagree on the list? We had this problem in America when the North and the South disagreed on the justice of slavery. In such a situation, who arbitrates?

John Stuart Mill took a utilitarian approach, suggesting that justice consists of the equal opportunities offered to people.[3] But is it inherently unjust to not have wealth distributed equally to all people? Abraham, Job, David, Solomon, and many others in the Bible were wealthy people. They prospered more than others. Was this unjust?

Other examples could be mentioned, but my purpose is not to review all the theories of justice ever proposed. My point is to show the flaw of starting a discussion on justice with man. Start with man and you end at varying conceptions of justice.

THE RIGHT STARTING POINT

The correct starting point of justice must be—and can only be—*God*. To gain a right understanding of justice, we must explore the relationship between three of His attributes—holiness, righteousness, and justice.

Holiness stands at the center; it is God's attribute that sets Him apart from all of His creation. That God is holy means He is intrinsically pure, without sin, free from any moral blemish, and has an "otherness" to His being. Holiness is not part of who God is; it's all of who God is. Tozer once said, "Holy is the way God is. To be holy He does not conform to a standard. He is that standard. He is absolutely holy with an infinite, incomprehensible fullness of purity that is incapable of being other than it is. Because He is holy, all His attributes are holy."[4]

God repeatedly reveals himself in the Bible as the Holy One. In the Law of Moses He said, "Speak to all the congregation of the people of Israel and say to them, You shall be holy, for I the LORD your God am holy" (Lev. 19:2). David ascribes holiness to God in the Psalms when he writes, "Yet you are holy, enthroned on the praises of Israel" (Ps. 22:3). The revelation given to John shows how God is worshipped for His holiness; the four living creatures before His throne never cease to say, "Holy, holy, holy, is the LORD God Almighty, who was and is and is to come!" (Rev. 4:8).

Righteousness and justice are closely linked to God's holiness and can be considered two sides to the same coin. We can't speak of one without speaking of the other. The Hebrew word for *righteousness* literally means "straight" or "right." That which is righteous is straight, as opposed to crooked.

I studied architecture in undergraduate school. Before the days of computer-aided design, we drew everything with pencil on paper. To ensure that my lines were straight, I had a T square, or a straight edge. In that sense my T square was "righteous," unlike a stick found in my yard, which would inevitably be crooked or "unrighteous."

To say God is righteous is to say that God is straight, right, and conforming to a standard. What is that standard? His holiness—His sinless and pure moral character. Where is that standard revealed? In His Word.

God is righteous, and He cannot and will not violate His holy character. King David makes this clear in one of his most beautiful psalms: "The law of the LORD is perfect, reviving the soul; the testimony of the LORD is sure, making wise the simple; the precepts of the LORD are *right*, rejoicing the heart" (Ps. 19:7–8a).

David says that the Word of God is right. He also says it is righteous: "The fear of the LORD is clean, enduring forever; the rules of the LORD are true, and *righteous* altogether" (Ps. 19:9). God's Word perfectly reflects His holy and righteous character.

Justice is closely related to God's righteousness; it is the out-working of that righteousness. God is just in that He requires us to conform to His righteousness and holiness. If we do so, He justly rewards us. If we don't, He justly punishes us.

The Bible shows us how God can never be guilty of injustice. In Genesis 18 an angel of the Lord tells Abraham that God is going to destroy the cities of Sodom and Gomorrah. Abraham's nephew, Lot, lives in the city of Sodom. The two cities were famous for their sexual depravity. Our term *sodomy* remains in use more than four thousand years later as a reminder of the violent homosexual activity present in those cities.

When God reveals these plans to Abraham, we might expect Abraham to respond with relief and righteous indignation, since he is aware of Sodom and Gomorrah's wickedness. But he doesn't. He asks God a series of questions, probing His justice. He asks, "Will you indeed sweep away the righteous with the wicked? Suppose there are fifty righteous within the city. Will you then sweep away the place and not spare it for the fifty righteous who are in it?" (Gen. 18:23–24).

Abraham is asking, "Is this right? Is this just? Yes, I know the wicked deserve to be punished, but it is right to punish the righteous along with them?"

I remember in junior high when our entire math class was forced to stay after school because someone in the class was misbehaving when the teacher's back was turned. I recognize that teaching math to a class of squirrely preadolescents can be worse than solitary confinement at San Quentin, but I also remember thinking that the sweeping detention didn't seem right. One person was guilty—but we were all being punished.

This is Abraham's point. He knows that God will not act unjustly. "Far be it from you to do such a thing, to put the righteous to death with the wicked, so that the righteous fare as the wicked! Far be that from you!" (Gen. 18:25a).

Abraham then drives the truth home: "Shall not the Judge

of all the earth do what is just?" (Gen. 18:25b). He asks a rhetorical question. Can the just Judge act unjustly? The answer is, of course, no. The Judge of the entire earth cannot act unjustly, because He is righteous. He will never do anything that is not right, just, and holy.

The relationship between these three attributes of God can be summarized like this:

- God is holy—*He is the moral standard.*
- God is righteous—*He conforms to the moral standard.*
- God is just—*He requires His creatures to likewise conform to the moral standard.*

WHAT IS JUSTICE?

If you have followed my argument so far, the reason different views of justice exist is obvious. Without a righteous standard of measurement, we can believe certain actions are straight when they are crooked.

Without a righteous standard of measurement, we can believe certain actions are straight when they are crooked.

My father worked in the lumber business for forty years, and I gained my first employment as a teenager at his company. During my years there, one of my duties was helping customers select their lumber. Professional contractors know how to lift up the edge of a stud, eyeball its edge, and see whether or not it was straight. Other people didn't have a clue. For them any board was straight, even if it was so crooked it could be used as a ski.

This variance in discernment is our dilemma when we start the pursuit of justice with man. Without a straight edge for a standard, anything and everything will look straight to somebody. That is not justice.

Justice is the application of God's righteous moral standards to the conduct of man. It starts with God, not man.

At most it's the appearance of justice. *Justice is the application of God's righteous moral standards to the conduct of man.* It starts with God, not man.

THE PURPOSE OF JUSTICE

If justice has its starting point with God and not with man, then the purpose of justice is determined by God, not man. To this end, we must also deal with two popular but wrong perceptions of why we enforce justice.

1. The purpose of justice is not to reform or rehabilitate an offender. In a man-centered justice system, reformation is often one of the goals. I don't deny reformation can and does occur, and I affirm that such life change can dramatically reduce recidivism. I also applaud the work of Prison Fellowship and other jail ministries that bring the gospel and powerful discipleship to incarcerated men and women. But reformation, while important, is not the purpose of a God-centered justice system.

2. The purpose of justice is not to suppress crime. In a man-centered system we generally assume the removal of criminals from society serves to warn others and also makes day-to-day life better on our streets. Potential criminals are deterred, and we feel safer.

This may indeed be true, but this misunderstands the purpose of justice.

Biblical justice is about sin's affront to God's holiness. Since sin falls short of our God's righteous standards, our holy God must punish sin. "For the wrath of God is revealed from heaven against all ungodliness and unrighteousness of men, who by their unrighteousness suppress the truth" (Rom. 1:18). God is angry about sin, and His justice requires Him to rightly punish sinners.

Jesus took sin's punishment for believers. "There is therefore now no condemnation for those who are in Christ Jesus" (Rom. 8:1). God's justice is perfectly satisfied by Jesus' work on the cross. While we were once stained by sin, thanks to Christ's atoning work God can now declare us righteous. When we sin we experience His discipline as a Father, which is restorative and redemptive. But that's not the purpose of justice.

If incarceration causes potential offenders to veer from sin and creates a safer society, those are welcome side benefits. If the threat of punishment leads some to pursue what is right and that results in quiet, tranquil communities, everyone wins. But the reduction of crime is not the purpose of justice. The purpose of justice is to uphold God's holy righteousness.

GOD'S IMPARTIAL JUSTICE

As fallen human beings we are deeply prone to partiality. I will dig into this in later chapters, but it bears mentioning here. Partiality is not new to the church; James spoke against it in his epistle: "My brothers, show no partiality as you hold the faith in our Lord Jesus Christ, the Lord of glory" (2:1). James then contrasts how a wealthy man dressed in designer duds is treated when entering the church versus a poor man in rags. Decisions are made based solely on each man's external appearance.

The context in James is partiality and judging in the church, but we all know that partiality is not limited to the assembly on Sunday. It happens on the streets of our cities, in the courtrooms across our country, and in every place where people mix. People are partial. I am. You are.

The encouraging word is that God is not partial. He is holy. He is righteous. He is the impartial Judge! While we quickly judge a person by external appearances, God is no respecter of persons. While we may be swayed by a person's position or prestige, God will not. If God were susceptible to partiality, we would expect Him to be favorable to the Jews—they are His chosen people. But Paul gives us these plain words: "For God shows no partiality" (Rom. 2:11).

Every person—without exception—stands on level ground before God's throne. R. C. Sproul puts it this way: "God does not respond to bribes or hear only the cases of the rich and powerful. He does not allow Lady Justice to peek from beneath her blindfold. . . . His scales are in balance."[5]

In our world the scales of justice are imbalanced. The hundreds of protestors who marched through Chicago chanting "Sixteen shots!" felt the scales were tipped against their community. At the time of writing, the Chicago court system was still sorting it all out. And I pray that justice is served. Yet until we orient our definition of justice to God's standard, we are left to measure with crooked sticks, which gets us nowhere.

Justice must begin with God. Only then can we start understanding our place in His justice.

CHAPTER 2

THE ROLE OF
MAN IN JUSTICE

The jury summons arrived in my office and demanded my participation. I was to appear at the Cook County Courthouse as part of a pool of potential candidates for a trial. I'd already been excused when a similar request appeared in my mail several years prior. I knew I had no way to avoid this summons. Despite the unwelcome disruption to my schedule, I grudgingly went.

Anticipating a boring day of waiting, I took a bag of work to the jury selection room. I'd barely turned on my computer when my group was called, and I trailed the others to the courtroom, confident that my role as a Bible college president would quickly eliminate me as a potential juror. I was stunned when I was selected.

I'd been reared watching *The Perry Mason Show* on our family's black-and-white TV, and as an adult I'd read my share of John Grisham novels. So I held a specific mental image of how the courtroom drama would play out: clear facts would emerge in the fog of ample plot twists, and the jury would rightly pronounce its just verdict.

Or so I thought. This trial was not some thirty-minute, scripted television show. This was the grit of real life. A defendant, smartly dressed in suit and tie, stood trial for a heinous crime against a young girl. Witnesses were called, evidence was introduced, and attorneys passionately pled their cases. At the end of the two-day trial, the twelve jurors were sequestered to render a decision. I realized the weight of our task. A man would be either freed or locked up for a long time based on our decision. I wondered about the words of Amos: "Let justice roll down like waters" (5:24). Was this how God wanted justice to roll?

> **A man would be either freed or locked up for a long time based on our decision.**

We saw in chapter one that justice begins with God. His holiness is the moral standard, and in His righteousness He never veers from that moral standard. True justice is the application of that moral standard to mankind. Justice begins with God, not man.

But man has a role in justice.

A tour through the Bible reveals an intentional progression in how justice is applied to man. In the earliest pages of the Old Testament we see God directly enforcing His righteous standards. Adam and Eve violated one of God's commands—not to eat from the tree of good and evil—and God pronounced judgment on them, the serpent, and all of creation (Gen. 3:14–19).

As man multiplied, so did sin. God was grieved by the wickedness of man and decided on a global judgment. "So the LORD said, 'I will blot out man whom I have created from the face of the land, man and animals and creeping things and birds of the heavens, for I am sorry that I have made them'" (Gen. 6:7). God washed away all mankind, save Noah and his family, in a flood.

At other times God used angels to announce His judgment

on man, while still acting directly. When the wretchedness of Sodom and Gomorrah become a stench before God, Abraham was greeted by two angels—appearing as men—who assessed the sin before declaring God's judgment (Gen. 18:21). While Lot and his family were spared, the infamous cities were pummeled. "Then the LORD rained on Sodom and Gomorrah sulfur and fire from the LORD out of heaven. And he overthrew those cities, and all the valley, and all the inhabitants of the cities, and what grew on the ground" (19:24–25).

God also judged the nation of Israel directly and repeatedly in their wilderness wanderings. The people griped. They complained. They yearned for the days when they were slaves in Egypt. God sent plagues, serpents, and a destroying angel. The most comprehensive judgment came when the nation rejected Caleb and Joshua's good report on the Promised Land and chose the ten spies' bad report (Num. 14). Over a million graves were dug in the sand over the next four decades to accommodate all those who would die without entering the land.

HUMAN JUDGES

Once in the land a noticeable transition occurred in the execution of justice—God instituted human judges. Spirit-filled men and women became the vehicles through which God judged His people.

Deborah was such a judge. Unlike those laden with military exploits—such as Gideon, Jephthah, or Samson—Deborah's role as a judge was more what we are used to: "She used to sit under the palm of Deborah between Ramah and Bethel in the hill country of Ephraim, and the people of Israel came up to her for judgment" (Judg. 4:5).

Deborah's courtroom was under a tree in the northern part of the land. People were apparently aware that she had the mind of God because they brought her their disputes from all over the country. We are not given examples, but we can easily imagine the conflicts. Who owns this property? Who is responsible for the loss of this donkey? What should be done to the poor man who steals bread? As a prophetess and a judge, Deborah provided true justice to the Israelites in their early days as a nation.

Years later, Samuel followed her as the last of the judges, when Israel was still a theocracy. The need for justice was increasing, so Samuel held court in several locations. He traveled on a circuit from his home in Ramah to Bethel, Gilgal, and Mizpah (1 Sam. 7:16). While Samuel was also a kingmaker—he anointed both Saul and David—his docket as judge was likely similar to Deborah's. As God's representative, he settled disputes and executed justice.

The breakdown in the execution of divine justice appeared with two of Samuel's sons, Joel and Abijah. Although raised in a godly home, they lacked the righteousness of their father. The text is indicting: "His sons did not walk in his ways but turned aside after gain. They took bribes and perverted justice" (1 Sam. 8:3).

When the verse says that the sons "turned aside" after gain and "perverted" justice, the same Hebrew verb is used. This word, when used in a literal sense elsewhere in the Old Testament, refers to something being altered from its original state—such as a shadow that is lengthened (see Jer. 6:4). When used to speak of a person's relationship with God, it refers to swerving or straying from the path of righteousness (see Prov. 4:27). In this description of Samuel's sons, both senses come through in the wordplay. They "turned aside" after gain (departing from the right path), and they "perverted" justice (changing it from its original shape or meaning).

Because of the sons' actions, the people rejected them as

judges. The elders of Israel came to Samuel at his home in Ramah and asked for a king to judge them (1 Sam. 8:5). The nation rightly wanted justice, and they thought they'd find it in a king. Unfortunately, most of their kings would go on to pervert justice, just as Samuel's sons had. But one king embodied justice considerably well, and his name was Solomon.

King Solomon was the rare exception because of God's special enablement. Because Solomon loved the Lord, shortly after he took the throne God appeared to him, saying, "Ask what I shall give you" (1 Kings 3:5). Instead of choosing riches or a long life, Solomon asked God for the wisdom to rightly judge the people: "Give your servant therefore an understanding mind to govern your people, that I may discern between good and evil" (v. 9). In short,

> **The nation rightly wanted justice, and they thought they'd find it in a king.**

Solomon asked for the ability to judge fairly and execute justice.

Proof that he received this wisdom immediately follows. Two prostitutes who shared a house brought their dispute before him. Both women had newborn sons born only days apart. One accidently suffocated her son during the night but shrewdly switched her dead son for the other woman's live son. When the wronged woman realizes the crime, a dispute erupted. They marched into Solomon's throne room, both claiming to be the real mother of the surviving son.

This was before DNA testing. This was before genetics could reliably identify the true parent. Two angry women, one innocent child.

Solomon asks for a sword. When he commands the baby to be split in two and a bloody half given to each woman, the love of the real mother emerges. She begs Solomon to give the child to the other woman and not kill him, while the second woman eagerly wants the boy to be killed. Solomon rightly awards the child to the first woman. When the nation heard of such great wisdom, they "stood in awe of the king, because they perceived that the wisdom of God was in him to *do justice*" (1 Kings 3:28).

That's a real judge. That's how justice was supposed to roll.

Unfortunately, the kingdom of Israel divided, and a parade of evil kings resided in the palace (especially in the northern kingdom). The prophets—who were the voice of God—called out the peoples' rampant injustice. Hear their words:

1. *Isaiah 3:14–15:* "The LORD will enter into judgment with the elders and princes of his people: 'It is you who have devoured the vineyard, the spoil of the poor is in your houses. What do you mean by crushing my people, by grinding the face of the poor?' declares the LORD God of hosts."

2. *Isaiah 10:1–2:* "Woe to those who decree iniquitous decrees, and the writers who keep writing oppression, to turn aside the needy from justice and to rob the poor of my people of their right, that widows may be their spoil, and that they may make the fatherless their prey!"

3. *Jeremiah 5:28:* "They know no bounds in deeds of evil; they judge not with justice the cause of the fatherless, to make it prosper, and they do not defend the rights of the needy."

4. *Amos 2:6–7a:* "For three transgressions of Israel, and for four, I will not revoke the punishment, because they sell the righteous for silver, and the needy for a pair of sandals —those who trample the head of the poor into the dust

of the earth and turn aside the way of the afflicted."

5. *Micah 2:1–2:* "Woe to those who devise wickedness and work evil on their beds! When the morning dawns, they perform it, because it is in the power of their hand. They covet fields and seize them, and houses, and take them away; they oppress a man and his house, a man and his inheritance."

That is *not* how justice was supposed to roll. Therefore, both kingdoms were judged by God for their injustice and banished to foreign lands.

HUMAN GOVERNMENT

In our age, God still intends for justice to be executed through human judges. While we are not living in a theocracy like Israel, God still seeks to extend common grace to us through the governing authorities. This was true even of godless emperors, for Paul writes in Romans 13:1–4:

Let every person be subject to the governing authorities. For there is no authority except from God, and those that exist have been instituted by God. Therefore, whoever resists the authorities resists what God has appointed, and those who resist will incur judgment. For rulers are not a terror to good conduct, but to bad. Would you have no fear of the one who is in authority? Then do what is good, and you will receive his approval, for he is God's servant for your good. But if you do wrong, be afraid, for he does not bear the sword in vain. For he is the servant of God, an avenger who carries out God's wrath on the wrongdoer.

Today God expects justice to be served through our government, leaders, and judges. It's not optional, even though we've noted how elusive it can be. Note the three vital points Paul makes in the above passage:

1. *The authority to judge comes from God, not from man (v. 1).*

Judges gain a right to the bench in different ways. Some, such as the justices of the US Supreme Court, are appointed to their position. Others are elected, such as those on the local level. But however a judge assumes his or her role, we cannot mistakenly assume that the citizens are bestowing the authority. All authority ultimately comes from God, who rules sovereignly over his creation (Ps. 103:19). He has simply delegated it to rulers and judges, making them accountable to Him whether they acknowledge it or not.

2. *Judges are servants of God (v. 4).*

Paul tells us that a ruler—and a judge—is "God's servant for your good." In the Bible the word *servant* often referred to civic leaders. God called Nebuchadnezzar, the king of Babylon, His servant in Jeremiah 25:9. The same is true of King Cyrus, the great Persian king (Isaiah 45:1). The New Testament term *servant* flowed into the church and designated both general servants of the assembly as well as an office of servants (deacons). In the same way, judges—and by extension all those involved in law enforcement—are servants of God. They derive their authority from Him and are to serve Him through the execution of their functions. Some, like Hitler or Sadaam Hussein, fail to rightly discharge their roles, but that doesn't negate the divine power behind their appointment.

3. Judges are to apply God's justice to the people (v. 3).

Remembering that justice begins with God and not with man, the role of man in justice is to rightly apply God's righteousness to man. Paul says that judges "are not a terror to good conduct, but to bad." Good behavior conforms with God and His holiness; bad behavior deviates from it. No other measuring stick can be allowed.

Once a human judge determines if conduct was good or bad, justice is to follow. "If you do wrong, be afraid, for he does not bear the sword in vain," and as God's servant he is "an avenger who carries out God's wrath on the wrongdoer" (v. 4). Don't miss the mention of God's wrath. *Wrath* is God's holy response against sin and unrighteousness (Rom. 1). God must judge sin. When He does, the Bible calls it His wrath.

Good behavior conforms with God and His holiness; bad behavior deviates from it. No other measuring stick can be allowed.

God expects human judges to carry out His wrath on evildoers. Sometimes, as with demise of Ananias and Sapphira (Acts 5:1–11), He directly intervenes in judgment. But normally God intends justice to be administered by the human agents He has appointed. Leaders are to discern if someone violates God's standard and execute justice. They are also to reward and honor those who do good: "Do what is good, and you will receive his approval" (Rom 13:3).

This is how God intends justice to roll. In the trial for which I served on the jury, the evidence seemed clear and a verdict was rendered. A group of twelve men and women weighed the facts, evaluated if there was a breach of our laws, and made a decision.

37

And a man's life was dramatically changed. Did he receive justice? I honestly don't know—and I won't know for certain until I arrive in heaven. As I've already shown—and as we are all aware—justice remains maddeningly elusive on this earth. Innocent men and women are sometimes punished. The guilty sometimes escape judgment. Justice fails to be executed. Mankind has our role in bringing justice to our world, but we are continually frustrated in our efforts and the efforts of those in authority. This is why it is helpful to understand the reasons justice remains elusive.

PART TWO

WHY IS JUSTICE ELUSIVE?

CHAPTER 3

THE LEGISLATIVE REASON: WE MAKE UNJUST LAWS

A young African American man named Dick Rowland needed to use the restroom. The year was 1921. The place was Tulsa, Oklahoma. Rowland was a shoe shiner who worked at a station on Main Street.

There was a restroom on the first floor of the building next door, but he was not permitted to use it. It was a whites-only bathroom. As a black man, Rowland was required by law to use only "colored" restrooms. Since the closest colored restroom was on the top floor of the building, he rode the elevator. Reports say that during the ride he accidently stepped on the toe of the elevator operator, a white teenager named Sarah Page. Rumors flew, and the stories expanded to claim that he had sexually assaulted her.

Rowland was arrested and dumped in jail awaiting a hearing. In the streets outside, a lynch mob formed to string him up. As things turned even surlier, a group of African Americans decided to protect their friend. A gunshot went off. A fight broke out. Things quickly escalated and a large crowd of "deputized" white residents marched through the black section of town, called Greenwood, and left destruction in their wake. In the end, more than one thousand homes of black families were torched, key black businesses were destroyed, and an unknown number of black citizens lost their lives.[1]

This disturbing story emerges from a time when Jim Crow laws ruled our land.[2] The days were messy after the Civil War and subsequent freeing of black slaves. Our nation failed to cleanly dispense of the racial prejudice and segregation deeply rooted in society—especially in the South. The Supreme Court ruled in 1896 (*Plessy v. Ferguson*) that "separate but equal" public facilities were required, segregating black people from white people in virtually all areas of public life. Drinking fountains, libraries, schools, and even restrooms—such as the one Rowland used in Tulsa—were clearly marked *Colored*. The ruling was overturned in 1954 by the Supreme Court in the landmark *Brown v. The Board of Education of Topeka*. Even with that legal precedent, the establishment of full, equal rights for African Americans has been bumpy and slow.

WHAT DEFINES INJUSTICE?

While nearly all Americans today are horrified by the Jim Crow laws, which gripped our land for nearly a century, this unsettling fact remains: for a long time we did not consider them unjust. We do now, *but we didn't then*. Since our definition of injustice rides a moving scale, the question must be asked: *What defines injustice?*

If justice is the application of God's righteous standards to our conduct, unjust laws impose legal requirements that are contrary to those divine standards—or give liberty to what God has forbidden. These laws may be legal according to the courts, but that doesn't make them just in the eyes of God or in conformity to the truths in His Word.

Martin Luther King Jr. concurred when he wrote his letter from a Birmingham jail in 1963:

> How does one determine when a law is just or unjust? A just law is a man-made code that squares with the moral law, or the law of God. An unjust law is a code that is out of harmony with the moral law. To put it in the terms of St. Thomas Aquinas, an unjust law is a human law that is not rooted in eternal and natural law.[3]

While nearly all Americans today are horrified by the Jim Crow laws, which gripped our land for nearly a century, this unsettling fact remains: for a long time we did not consider them unjust.

This, then, is the plumb line. Unjust laws are legal codes that deviate from God's Word. One reason justice remains elusive today is that we have made—and continue to make—unjust laws.

UNJUST LAWS IN THE PAST

I don't wish to shame us here; American society is no different than any other in the world when it comes to the establishment of unjust laws. Because of our Judeo-Christian heritage, we may enjoy more justice than many parts of the world. But in addition to the infamous Jim Crow Laws, we have had our share of other laws that stood opposed to God's Word.

The Fugitive Slave Acts (1793; 1850)

The Fugitive Slave Acts were federal laws allowing the capture and return of runaway slaves within the territory of the United States. The 1793 Act authorized local governments to seize and return escaped slaves to their owners and imposed penalties on anyone who aided in a slave's flight. This law was amended and strengthened by the Fugitive Slave Act of 1850. The second Act added further provisions for tracking down runaways and levied even harsher punishments for interfering in their capture. Both Acts were abolished by Congress in 1864 after the passage of the Thirteenth Amendment.

These two Acts contradicted the Bible, which affirms the dignity and equality of every human being. Everyone—regardless of skin color, gender, or ethnicity—has value because of God's image stamped on them (Gen. 1:26). In Psalm 8 David writes concerning man, "Yet you have made him a little lower than the heavenly beings and crowned him with glory and honor. You have given him dominion over the works of your hands; you have put all things under his feet" (vv. 5–6). In God's eyes, every person on the planet has inherent value and has been bestowed with honor and dignity—despite the bigoted efforts of some to erase it.

Thankfully, some people saw the injustice of the Fugitive Slave Acts. Despite the threat of prosecution and punishment, the Underground Railroad was created to help runaway slaves gain freedom. Some of the leaders in this movement were Reverend Samuel and Florella Adair—a clergy couple in Kansas—and Florella's brother, John Brown. The Adairs' small log cabin still stands in northeast Kansas as a marker of the Underground Railroad's impact on history, complete with the room where they hid slaves.

The "Ugly" Laws (1880s)

As urban centers across the country swelled in the late nineteenth century—due in large part to the rise in immigrant populations—cities sought to regulate the increasing numbers of impoverished people on their congested streets. The "ugly" laws were passed in many municipalities to ban the poor, crippled, and unseemly from visibility.

In 1867 San Francisco became the first to pass such an ordinance. Other cities followed suit. My hometown of Omaha had one. My present city of Chicago passed a law in 1881 that read as follows:

> Whereas the streets and sidewalks of the City of Chicago contain numerous beggars, mendicants, organ-grinders and other unsightly and unseemly objects, which are a reproach to the City, disagreeable to people upon the streets, an offense to business houses along the streets and often dangerous, Therefore it be ordered, That the mayor at once take steps to remove from the streets all beggars, mendicants, and all those who by way of making Exhibition of themselves and their infirmaries seek to obtain money from people on and along the streets.[4]

In most cases, offenders faced incarceration or fines.

While not regularly enforced, most of these laws were not repealed until the 1970s. Chicago officially voted to repeal its law in 1974. The Americans with Disabilities Act (ADA) of 1990 eliminated the legality of any "ugly" laws that still persisted. As we noted in chapter two, God has an abiding concern for the poor and needy. Instead of banishing them from our sight, we are to show compassion for the most vulnerable of society.

The Racial Integrity Act (1924)

The Racial Integrity Act was passed in Virginia to protect "whiteness" against what many Virginians perceived to be the negative effects of mixing races. This Act prohibited interracial marriage and defined a white person as one who had no trace of any blood but Caucasian. It utilized the "one drop rule,"[5] classifying as "colored" anyone who had even one drop of African or Native American blood in their veins. This law remained in force until the US Supreme Court overturned it in 1967 (*Loving v. Virginia*).

This Act represented sinful white supremacy and denied the biblical doctrine of the equality of all human beings. Speaking to the church, Paul wrote, "There is neither Jew nor Greek, there is neither slave nor free, there is no male or female, for you are all one in Christ Jesus" (Gal. 3:28). In a vivid display of the equality of all races, the book of Revelation contains a song that will be sung before the Lamb's throne: "Worthy are you to take the scroll and to open its seals, for you were slain, and by your blood you ransomed people for God from every tribe and language and people and nation, and you have made them a kingdom of priests to our God" (5:9–10). Every people group—regardless of blood type—has been ransomed by the blood of Jesus. Instead of a posture of pride and supremacy, our correct posture should be one of humility and celebration.

The Virginia Sterilization Act (1924)

This law was passed in the same state and in the same year as the Racial Integrity Act. Riding the wave of a eugenics movement—designed to protect the purity of the American race—this program practiced forced sterilization. It deemed certain people unfit or unworthy to procreate, so they were required to be sterilized. Included in this list of undesirables were patients at state mental institutions, those with physical deformities, the feeble-minded, and even the homeless. Most victims were women, and many were not told that they were being sterilized. While firm numbers are not available, an estimated 7,200–8,300 people were sterilized between 1927 and 1979.[6] Curiously, this Act was never declared unconstitutional by the Virginia General Assembly, although in 2015 they voted to compensate the sterilized individuals.

In contrast to this Act, the Bible declares that God controls the womb and he intimately knows every child's formation.

> For you formed my inward parts; you knitted me together in my mother's womb. I praise you, for I am fearfully and wonderfully made. . . . My frame was not hidden from you, when I was being made in secret, intricately woven in the depths of the earth. Your eyes saw my unformed substance; in your book were written, every one one of them, the days that were formed for me, when as yet there was none of them. (Ps. 139:13–16)

It is unjust and blasphemous for man to assume the role of God in determining who can and cannot have children. Children "are a heritage from the LORD" (Ps. 127:3).

UNJUST LAWS IN THE PRESENT

I wish I could say that all unjust laws are in our past. I'd like to be able to state that here in America we no longer pass unjust laws. But we do. Here are a few prominent examples.

Roe v. Wade (1973)

You know this landmark case, when the US Supreme Court chose to elevate the rights of the mother over the rights of the unborn child. Officially, it determined that a state law banning abortions was unconstitutional (except to save the life of the mother). The court also ruled that states were forbidden from outlawing or regulating any aspect of abortion performed during the first trimester of pregnancy. States could only enact abortion regulations in the second and third trimesters if those regulations were reasonably related to maternal health.

God declares that all life is sacred and to be zealously protected. We already saw God's loving and sovereign involvement with unborn children in Psalm 139. David also shows that life begins at the moment of conception when he writes, "Behold, I was brought forth in iniquity, and in sin did my mother conceive me" (Ps. 51:5). He is explaining that he possessed a sin nature from the moment he was conceived, and thus he was morally culpable at that moment and—by necessity—possessed personhood.

Powerful evidence of this is also seen in the sequence surrounding the conceptions of Jesus and John the Baptist (Luke 1). John is miraculously conceived in Luke 1:24, even though both of his parents, Zechariah and Elizabeth, are beyond normal childbearing years. Jesus is miraculously conceived in Mary by the Holy Spirit shortly after Gabriel's visit in verses 26–38.

Mary travels from Galilee to Judea to visit her cousin Elizabeth, perhaps in part to escape the community stigma of her condition. When Mary greets her, Luke reports that the baby in Elizabeth's womb "leaped for joy" (v. 44). The forerunner in Elizabeth's womb recognized the Messiah in Mary's. How long had Mary been pregnant at this point? Probably only a few weeks—

she was certainly in her first trimester. Yet even then the Bible recognizes the full personhood of both babies.

Roe v. Wade is an unjust law. It is contrary to God's Word and denies the sanctity of human life. Unfortunately—to our shame—it has remained in force for more than four decades in the bloody shadow of fifty-six million abortions.

Obergefell v. Hodges (2015)

You may not recognize the official title of this ruling when the US Supreme Court made same-sex marriage a federal law. Before this ruling, individual states had legalized gay marriage, but other states had banned it. After this decision, which was a controversial 5–4 vote, gay marriage became a constitutional right.

This is an unjust law because it arrogantly dismisses biblical marriage. God created man and woman, and God also instituted marriage for all mankind—between a man and a woman. Genesis 2:24 gives us this lasting instruction: "Therefore a man shall leave his father and his mother and hold fast to his wife, and they shall become one flesh." This truth is also reflected in the mysterious union between Christ and His church. Christ is the Bridegroom; the church is His bride (Eph. 5:31–32).

The Bible also directly condemns homosexual behavior. In Leviticus 18:22 God clearly says, "You shall not lie with a male as with a woman; it is an abomination." Paul explains in Romans 1 that such behavior is a perversion of the natural order: "For this reason God gave them up to dishonorable passions. For their women exchanged natural relations for those that are contrary to nature; and the men likewise gave up natural relations with women and were consumed with passion for one another, men committing shameless acts with men and receiving in themselves the due penalty for their error" (Rom. 1:26–27).

The legalization of gay marriage does not make it just. The court can make anything legal, but only conformity with God's Word determines if it's just.

The court can make anything legal, but only conformity with God's Word determines if it's just.

Physician-Assisted Suicide Laws

Since 1994 five states have legalized physician-assisted suicide (Oregon, Washington, Montana, Vermont, and California). The structure of these laws is nearly identical, with each requiring a terminally ill patient to submit three requests to the physician within the last (anticipated) six months of the patient's life. In such cases, a medical doctor can with impunity assist a patient with the planning and execution of his or her own death—usually with the prescription of deadly doses of a drug.

Beyond the violation of the Hippocratic Oath that this act represents, it also violates God's Word. Life is a gift from God (Ps. 127:3), and only He can determine when it should end. As with abortion, these laws ignore the image of God that is stamped on each person and is not nullified even when suffering through a terminal disease. While it is not the norm, the same God who created the universe and raised Christ from the dead is more than able to bring healing to our most desperate situations. Physician-assisted suicide laws are unjust laws giving man authority that only God has.

Immigrant Deportation Laws

With an estimated 11.5 million undocumented workers in America, our country faces a complex immigration problem.

Concerns about terrorism and security complicate a deeply human issue. A maze of state and federal laws require the deportation of illegal immigrant parents, leaving children behind to navigate painful separations, foster homes, and detention centers. These children—if born in the United States—cannot leave, as they are not citizens of the country to which their parents are being deported.

The Bible declares that we are to make provision for the foreigners among us. "Love the sojourner, therefore, for you were sojourners in the land of Egypt" (Deut. 10:19). The Law of Moses declares that "When a stranger sojourns with you in your land, you shall not do him wrong. You shall treat the stranger who sojourns with you as the native among you, and you shall love him as yourself, for you were strangers in the land of Egypt; I am the LORD your God" (Lev. 19:33–34). Immigrants matter to God. How we treat immigrants matters to God. Deportation laws that rip children from their parents are not just.

If this chapter has proved anything, it's that we obstruct our own pursuit of justice by creating unjust laws. Yes, justice is elusive, but regarding legislation it is more accurate to say that we cast justice away, not that it gets away from us. When we pass laws contradicting God's Word, we won't realize justice. Instead we create a badly conflicted environment where legality isn't linked to justice,

> **We obstruct our own pursuit of justice by creating unjust laws.**

and in such a world we can settle for what is legal while missing what we desire most. We are the blind leading the blind.

CHAPTER 4

THE COGNITIVE REASON: WE HAVE LIMITED KNOWLEDGE

Joseph Green Brown faced two difficult adjustments in 1987. The first was being able to open and close a door at will. The second was putting on a seat belt.

Both actions would seem normal and natural to anyone who had lived a life of freedom. But Brown had spent fourteen-and-a-half years on death row in Florida. Convicted on a murder charge in 1974, he had not opened a door for himself in over a decade. Prison guards had always opened and closed the doors to his six-by-eight cell.

He was also squeamish about being belted down because he had fought for years against being strapped into the electric chair. His execution date had been set for October 18, 1983. The governor had signed his death warrant. Brown had even been measured for his burial suit. Just fifteen hours—nine hundred minutes!—before his execution, the US Court of Appeals for the Eleventh District reversed the conviction. The efforts of a private practice attorney—Richard Blumenthal, who later became the Attorney General and then a Senator of Connecticut—proved that the state's main witness against Brown had lied and now recanted his

Wilson was given a life sentence—*for stealing less than two dollars.*

story. The prosecutor's office chose not to seek a new trial, and Brown finally walked free in 1987—exonerated, but facing extraordinary physical, emotional, and spiritual adjustments after years of confinement staring down a date with death.[1]

In our human justice system, we don't know what we don't know. We investigate to discover the facts. We are as thorough as we can be within the limitations of our resources. We ask questions, depose witnesses, pursue theories, and build cases. But we don't know what we don't know. It's a sad consequence of our humanity—we have limited knowledge.

In many spheres of life, limited knowledge has minimal practical impact. If I buy oranges at one grocery store for $1.49 a pound unaware that another store had them on sale for $0.89 a pound, I am out a couple bucks, but it has no significant effect on my life. Or if I take my regular route to the airport unaware that an accident on the road has caused miles of gridlock, I may be rushed to catch my plane, but I can adjust.

In contrast, when it comes to legal justice issues, our limited knowledge has immense impact. Decisions are rendered, people are convicted, and lives are forever marked. Because of our inadequate knowledge, not only do we punish the innocent—like Joseph Green Brown—but we also acquit the guilty. Furthermore, we can dictate inappropriate punishment for an offense. Sometimes we're too lenient. Other times we're too harsh. Both extremes represent injustice.

Mary Dudziak tells the sordid tale of a young black man named Jimmy Wilson who was sentenced to death in Alabama in 1957 for an admitted crime.[2] But the crime was not murder or anything that might merit capital punishment. Wilson stole $1.95 from a white woman he worked for occasionally.

The trial took less than five hours. The all-white jury spent less than an hour discussing the case. Wilson was convicted of the crime and sentenced to death. His conviction was appealed to the Alabama Supreme Court, which upheld the decision. This travesty of justice brought outrage and protests from all four corners of the world, and placed intense pressure on then-governor James Folsom to intervene and grant clemency. Even the *Birmingham Post-Herald* came out in support of clemency, saying in an editorial that such a decision "would serve not only justice, but also the best interest of Alabama as well. . . . So much world-wide interest has been centered in this case and misunderstanding of it is widespread. . . . The sentence of death, if carried out, could never be satisfactorily explained much less justified before world opinion."[3]

Folsom complied to the overwhelming demand and granted Wilson clemency, letting the parole board determine the length of his sentence. In a stunning development, Wilson was given a life sentence—*for stealing less than two dollars*. After serving sixteen years he was finally paroled in 1973 at the age of seventy.

THE AID OF SCIENCE

Today our legal system has access to more information than ever before thanks to advances in science, particularly DNA testing. Dr. Francis H. C. Crick and Dr. James D. Watson's history-changing discovery of the double-helix DNA structure in 1953 has found application in many venues, including forensic science. First used in a courtroom in England in 1986, DNA analysis can determine matches between the defendant and physical evidence retrieved at a crime scene or from a victim, such as hair, blood, skin cells, or semen.

DNA testing in American courtrooms has led to the exoneration of more than three hundred people, twenty of whom were on death row. Every state except Maine, North Dakota, Rhode Island, and Utah allows for the admission of DNA evidence. As a result, every year the wrongfully convicted are released from prison.

Half-brothers Henry McCollum and Leon Brown are among those who have been freed. The two brothers, who both have mental limitations, were arrested in 1984 for the brutal rape and murder of an eleven-year-old girl. Although no physical evidence directly tied them to the scene of the crime, after five long hours of interrogation without the presence of a lawyer they both signed a confession. During the trial they claimed that they were innocent and said they only confessed under extreme duress. Brown was convicted of rape and received a life sentence. McCollum was convicted of both rape and murder and sent to death row.

In 2010, DNA evidence introduced to the court proved the two brothers' innocence and identified a different perpetrator. In 2014 the brothers finally gained their freedom—after serving thirty years for a crime that they didn't commit.[4]

Analysis of the cases exonerated by DNA evidence repeatedly reveals the fallibility of our knowledge.[5] A disturbing percentage of wrongful convictions—around 70 percent—come from misidentification by eyewitnesses. The witnesses think that they are identifying the perpetrator, but they make mistakes. Often a mistake is made when the witness is identifying a person of a different race; studies show that people are less able to recognize those of a race different from their own.

False confessions, such as the one signed by Brown and McCollum, are another leading reason for wrongful convictions.

This is the leading reason in cases involving homicide, as law enforcement officials often intensify interrogations in an effort to solve crimes. Another factor is the use of jailhouse informants and others given incentive to testify. Such persons can give information that is simply not true. But we don't know it's not true.

TRUE JUSTICE

The consistent application of true justice is impossible for us as human beings because we will *never*, in this life, have access to all the facts. Our creaturely limits hinder us from understanding all that there is to know about a situation.

Joshua, the fresh new leader of the nation of Israel, faced this dilemma in Joshua 7. Jericho lay in ruins and Israel's leaders prepared for their next conquest of a much less imposing target: the city of Ai. According to Joshua 8, Ai was not a large city. If you included every adult, both men and women, it numbered only twelve thousand people. If half of these were men, and if half of the men were able to fight, the king of Ai could have mustered an army of at most three thousand soldiers.

Israel's forces were much larger. Spurred by the confidence of conquering the much-larger Jericho, Joshua heeded the advice of his spies who surveyed Ai and sent an army of three thousand men into battle. They marched out expecting an easy victory— but they returned in devastating defeat. "They fled before the men of Ai, and the men of Ai killed about thirty-six of their men and chased them before the gate as far as Shebarim and struck them at the descent" (Josh. 7:4–5).

Devastating. Not only did Israelite soldiers lose their lives, but also the rest of the nation lost their courage—"the hearts of the people melted and became as water" (7:5).

Joshua was dumbfounded. He couldn't understand how Israel could go from military success to military failure so quickly. And as the nation's leader, he bore great grief, confusion, and even anger. He tore his clothes in mourning, put dust on his head, and fell flat on his face before God with accusing prayers:

Alas, O Lord GOD, why have you brought this people over the Jordan at all, to give us into the hands of the Amorites, to destroy us? Would we have been content to dwell beyond the Jordan! O Lord, what can I say, when Israel has turned their backs before their enemies! For the Canaanites and all the inhabitants of the land will hear of it and will surround us and cut off our name from the earth. And what will you do for your great name? (Josh. 7:7–9)

Joshua's questions reveal his lack of knowledge. He didn't know why Israel suffered such a great defeat, and he couldn't unless God told him. And God does. "Get up!" God says. "Why have you fallen on your face? Israel has sinned; they have transgressed my covenant that I commanded them; they have taken some of the devoted things; they have stolen and lied and put them among their own belongings" (vv. 10–11).

Israel had sinned. Not all Israel—just one man out of the thirty-thousand-man army that defeated Jericho. That one man who gained an infamous place in biblical history: Achan. He secretly took things God had placed under a ban. Joshua couldn't have known about the crime because he couldn't be aware of every action of every person in the nation.

But God supernaturally intervened and guided Joshua to identify Achan through casting lots, which led to a confession and the proper execution of justice. Achan was first stoned to death.

Then he was burned with fire. Finally, he was buried under a heap of stones.

MURDER OVER A VINEYARD

A similar story occurred in the days of Elijah (1 Kings 21). The notorious King Ahab was ruling on the throne of the northern kingdom of Israel. One day, as Ahab sauntered around the terrace of his palace in Jezreel, he noticed the nice vineyard of his neighbor, Naboth. He coveted the vineyard as a convenient place to grow his vegetables and made Naboth a reasonable offer to: (1) trade his vineyard for a more-distant but superior plot, or (2) sell the vineyard for cash.

Naboth flatly refused. The property was his family's inheritance in the land and, in compliance with the Law of Moses, it wasn't for sale. Ahab was used to getting what he wanted, so he pouted. He marched to his room, plopped on his bed, and refused to talk to anybody.

When his wife—the wicked queen Jezebel—uncovered the reason for Ahab's despondency, she crafted an evil plot to gain Naboth's vineyard. She needed to find a way to eliminate Naboth and his sons, and she found one. Committing forgery, she sent letters in the name of the king to the Jezreel city officials. Promoting perjury, she instructed the officials to hire a pair of so-called informants to accuse Naboth of two serious crimes during a citywide fast: blasphemy against God and treason against the king. Based on those fallacious testimonies, the kangaroo court was to render its verdict, and Naboth was to be taken outside the city and stoned to death.

The crime was committed. The city officials followed in lockstep with Jezebel's plan. A fast was proclaimed. Naboth was set up. Two lying witnesses accused him in court. The sentence was passed. By the end of the day, Naboth and his sons were dead. According to the custom of the day, the land of criminals reverted to the throne. Ahab now had the land for his vegetable garden. With glee he scurried down to take possession.

But God saw the crime. He is aware of every injustice because He is omniscient and omnipresent. The Bible repeatedly declares this truth. "Behold, you have sinned against the LORD, and be sure your sin will find you out" (Num. 32:23). "The eyes of the LORD are in every place, keeping watch on the evil and the good" (Prov. 15:3). "'Can a man hide himself in secret places so that I cannot see him?' declares the LORD. 'Do I not fill heaven and earth?' declares the LORD" (Jer. 23:24). God sees all; nothing gets past Him.

God knew about the crime committed against Naboth, and He sent Elijah to declare just judgment on the king. Meeting Ahab on the same blood-stained garden plot, Elijah announced sweeping judgment. Ahab would die. His seventy sons would die. Jezebel would die and, fittingly, become dog food.

The judgment was executed during the reign of King Jehu. The sons of Ahab were killed and, in a gruesome scene, their heads were piled in two heaps at the city gates. Jezebel had just finished putting on her makeup when she was shoved through her palace window to the streets below. She died, and the dogs had a feast.

Ahab's judgment puts a different twist on this story. When he learned of his judgment, he humbled himself before God. "When Ahab heard those words, he tore his clothes and put sackcloth on his flesh and fasted and lay in sackcloth and went about dejectedly" (1 Kings 21:27). This was Ahab's death row experience.

Like Joseph Green Brown, Ahab gained a reprieve, but not because he was innocent. He escaped the prescribed judgment because of God's abundant mercy. God said to Elijah, "Have you seen how Ahab has humbled himself before me? Because he has humbled himself before me, I will not bring the disaster in his days; but in his son's days I will bring disaster upon his house" (v. 29).

If we had been assigned to judge Ahab, we would have probably executed him. His reign was marked with continuous abominable acts and blatant idol worship. "Ahab the son of Omri did evil in the sight of the LORD, more than all who were before him" (16:30), and "Ahab did more to provoke the LORD, the God of Israel, to anger than all the kings of Israel who were before him" (v. 33).

But we don't know what we don't know. Only God has all the facts, and only God can see into the heart of man. He can do only what is just, as Abraham declared to his angelic visitor, "Far be it from you to do such a thing, to put the righteous to death with the wicked, so that the righteous fare as the wicked! Far be that from you! Shall not the Judge of all the earth do what is just?" (Gen. 18:25). Yes,

We don't know what we don't know.

He will do what is just—even with an unsavory figure like Ahab.

One significant reason justice remains elusive is that, unlike the omniscient God, we will always battle limited knowledge. As one researcher aptly put it, "People just cannot see what they are missing."[6] Richard Blumenthal, the attorney who took up the cause of Joseph Green Brown and provided the initial energy leading to his exoneration, recognized this vulnerability when he said, "An innocent man may be executed even in one of the fairest and most accurate systems of justice ever known."[7]

Our law enforcement teams can—and do—work diligently to discover the facts. Our legal teams can—and do—prepare well-reasoned arguments for their clients. Our forensic teams can—and do—seek to utilize the best and latest science in their investigations. Our judges and juries can—and do—seek to discern truth and make right decisions in the morass of conflicting data. But we can—and do—fail even in the midst of our best efforts.

Awareness of our limitations can prompt us to take a cue from Joshua and fall flat on our faces before the One with limitless knowledge. Only with His guidance can we work toward true justice.

CHAPTER 5

THE SPIRITUAL REASON:
WE HAVE DARKENED UNDERSTANDING

Three juries in three trials convicted Juan Rivera of the murder of 11-year-old Holly Staker in Waukegan, Illinois. But despite being convicted three times, Rivera was innocent. In fact, law enforcement records showed that it was impossible for him to have committed the crime.

The murder occurred on August 17, 1992, when Staker was babysitting for several neighborhood children at 442 Hickory Street. Acting on a tip from an informant, investigators identified Rivera as a likely suspect. Rivera, nineteen years old at the time and a special education student, denied knowledge of the crime during four days of intense questioning. At the end of the fourth day, Rivera broke down and indicated with a nod of his head that he committed the rape and murder. Distraught and confused, Rivera began beating his head against the walls of his padded cell. Later a nurse found him huddled on the floor in a fetal position. At 8 a.m. the next morning, he signed a confession the investigators had typed up for him, which was so rife with inconsistencies that it had to be revised. A few hours later, he signed a second confession.

In his first trial in 1993, Rivera was convicted and sentenced to life in prison without parole. But the Illinois Appellate Court reversed the conviction in 1996 because of improper rulings by the judge in the case. Rivera was tried again before the same judge two years later and again convicted, receiving an identical sentence. This conviction was vacated after new DNA evidence contradicted conclusions from the trial. He was tried on the same charge before the same judge a third time in 2009. Again Rivera was convicted, and again he was sentenced to life in prison without parole.

Rivera's case eventually gained the attention of lawyers and law professors alert to potentially wrongful convictions. When his conviction was appealed, it was reversed and the appellate court justices spoke harshly of the evidence-twisting that the court allowed. Two compelling distortions were evident.

First, the court dismissed the evidence from DNA testing that eliminated Rivera as a possible suspect. Second, they overlooked law enforcement records showing that it was impossible for him to commit the crime.

Because of an earlier conviction of burglary, Rivera was wearing an electronic monitoring device that showed his precise physical location at all times. Where was he at the time of the Staker rape and murder? According to police records, he was at his home more than two miles from the scene of the crime.

Despite this evidence Rivera was convicted three times and served nineteen years for a crime he did not commit—nor was physically able to commit! He was finally released from the Stateville Correctional Center on January 6, 2012.

It is one thing to recognize that we have limited knowledge. It is quite another to realize that we can twist and distort the facts that we do possess. Yet it happens—like it did with Juan Rivera. And like it did for Daniel Taylor.

Taylor was seventeen-years-old on December 3, 1992, when he was arrested and charged with the November 16 shooting deaths of Sharon Haugabook and Jeffery Lassiter on Chicago's North Side. Shortly after Taylor's arrest, two teenagers were arrested on drug charges. They confessed to participation in the murders and also implicated five others—including Taylor. After an interrogation, each of the five confessed, implicating the others.

But clear evidence showed that—despite Taylor's confession—it was physically impossible for him to be guilty because he was in police custody at the time of the murders. The murders occurred at 8:43 p.m. Taylor had been arrested for disorderly conduct at 6:45 p.m., and he was not released until 10 p.m.

Despite these facts, the prosecution alleged the police records were inaccurate because a drug dealer claimed to have seen Taylor on the street when he was allegedly in custody. Based almost exclusively on this testimony and Taylor's confession, a jury found him guilty, and Taylor was sentenced to life in prison.

Taylor's exoneration began when the *Chicago Tribune* started an investigation of his case in 2001. Proceedings continued for years until a sworn statement from the lockup keeper on duty on November 16 declared that it was not possible for Taylor to have been released before 10 p.m. and the drug dealer recanted his story. Faced with this new evidence, the charges against Taylor were dropped, and he was released on June 28, 2013, after spending more than two decades behind bars.

THE EFFECT OF SIN

These stories—and many others like them—can cause us to scratch our heads. How can intelligent, reasonable people overlook and distort evidence? How can facts be reshaped to fit a narrative that simply isn't true?

The Bible gives us the answer: we all have a darkened understanding. Our minds, hearts, and reason have been tragically twisted by sin. Paul explains this in Ephesians 4:17–18 when he says that unbelievers walk "in the futility of their minds" and "are darkened in their understanding" because "of the ignorance that is in them, due to their hardness of heart."

We are all sinners. Four key phrases in the above verses show the deep distortion caused by sin.

1. We have "futile minds" unable to perform in the way God intended.
2. We have "darkened understanding." Our reasoning processes lack clarity and definition.
3. We have "ignorance," a lack of normal perception or understanding.
4. We have "hard hearts." The center of our being, which contains our mind, will, and understanding, is not soft and malleable. It is hard as stone.

These facts are not true of just some people, such as psychopaths. They are true of all of us. "For all have sinned and fall short of the glory of God" (Rom. 3:23). We all have been distorted by sin, and we all live in a world marred by sin. Philosopher Nicholas Wolterstorff once said that "In this world of ours, things are often malformed, they often malfunction; they do not work according to their nature. This is true of human beings with respect to, among other things, their desires and inclinations; often those are disordered, malformed, unnatural."[1]

Because of sin's effect on our minds, we perceive things but our concept of truth may not correspond with reality. As Wolterstorff said, things are "often malformed."

Take for example the main office doors into Crowell Hall at Moody Bible Institute, where I serve. To allow in both natural and artificial light, the wooden doors to the offices have frosted glass inserts. The glass allows light to enter, but someone outside is unable to clearly see

We all have been distorted by sin, and we all live in a world marred by sin.

through the door. They can discern activity and see when someone is in the office, but little else. The glass is frosted. It prevents deeper comprehension of what is happening on the other side of the door. Sin has frosted our minds.

King Solomon, as he reflected on the state of man, said, "See, this alone I found, that God made man upright, but they have sought out many schemes" (Eccl. 7:29). When God made man, he declared it was all "very good" (Gen. 1:31). But when the serpent deceived Eve and sin entered the world, man was no longer upright. Ever since, man has "sought out many schemes." "The heart is deceitful above all things, and desperately sick; who can understand it?" (Jer. 17:9). We do not have a natural inclination toward what is right and true. We have a downward propensity to what is corrupt and evil. Even when we think we might be involved in good and desirable behavior free from anything sinful, our actions are still tainted—frosted by sin.

DARKENED JUDGES

This frosted, darkened understanding leads to darkened judges, who may wish to do right but whose minds are clouded. The result can be painfully damaging. Scripture gives us many examples of the wreckage from unjust judges.

The prophet Micah ministered during the reigns of Jotham, Ahaz, and Hezekiah in the southern kingdom of Judah, about seven hundred years before the birth of Christ. These were days of rampant corruption and injustice in the land, so Micah rails against the leaders and rulers:

> Hear, you heads of Jacob and rulers of the house of Israel! Is it not for you to know justice?—you who hate the good and love the evil, who tear the skin from off my people and their flesh from off their bones, who eat the flesh of my people, and flay their skin from off them, and break their bones in pieces and chop them up like meat in a pot, like flesh in a cauldron. . . . Hear this, you heads of the house of Jacob and rulers of the house of Israel, who detest justice and make crooked all that is straight. (Mic. 3:1–3, 9)

The description of the injustice is graphic. Like an unconcerned butcher, the rulers were chopping up the poor to drive them from their lands. Micah claims in verse 1 that these leaders should "know justice." But he says that instead they "hate the good and love the evil," with the word *hate* signaling a strong emotional revulsion, as if one was nauseated. With this reversed passion, they ground up the people until nothing was left. The poor were skinned, broken, and dropped in a boiling pot.

In verse 9 Micah makes two charges against the judges and

rulers. First he says that they "detest justice." Instead of seeing justice as an honorable goal to be pursued as God's representatives, it is abominable to them—offensive and abhorrent.

Second, Micah states that such judges "make crooked all that is straight." Remember the definition of righteousness? It means "that which is straight," while unrighteousness means "that which is crooked." In a scathing denunciation of these rulers, the prophet claims that they have effectively taken the things which are straight—the righteous things—and made them crooked, or unrighteous.

Sin hardens the heart and darkens the mind. Instead of pursuing what is right, we seek after what serves our own best interests. Facts are ignored, evidence is twisted, and justice is perverted. Furthermore, the crooked path doesn't look crooked—it seems straight.

The crooked path doesn't look crooked—it seems straight.

One of Micah's contemporaries was the greatest of all the prophets—Isaiah. He walked the same streets and witnessed the same injustices. In righteous anger Isaiah cried out, "Woe to those who decree iniquitous decrees, and the writers who keep writing oppression, to turn aside the needy from justice and to rob the poor of my people of their right, that widows may be their spoil, and that they may make the fatherless their prey!" (Isa. 10:1–2).

Isaiah explains that the ones in Judah responsible for writing new laws or enforcing existing ones were doing so in a way that padded their own bank accounts. The most needy—the widows and orphans—were not protected but preyed upon. Their few possessions were stripped away as the booty of the rich and powerful.

Sin twists us like that. Our perverse self-centeredness takes a calloused view to the needs of others and drives us to render judgments and decisions that wander far from what is right. This is why good King Jehoshaphat gave a stern warning to the judges he appointed in the fortified cities of Judah. "Consider what you do, for you judge not for man, but for the LORD. He is with you in giving judgment. . . . Be careful what you do, for there is no injustice with the LORD our God, or partiality or taking bribes" (2 Chron. 19:6–7). Judges are not immune from the pull toward injustice.

THE UNJUST JUDGE

Jesus tells the story of an unjust judge in Luke 18. The parable was meant to encourage His disciples to not lose heart in their prayers. It has two colorful characters. The first is a widow, who represents one of the most vulnerable in that society. Without a financial safety net, and apparently without any children to care for her, she is forced to fend for herself.

The second character is a judge: a prominent, powerful man who sits at the gates of the city and adjudicates disputes. Jesus gives us a glimpse into the judge's character when He says of him, "[He] neither feared God nor respected man" (18:2). He lacks a reverence for God as well as compassion for others. Picture a well-protected bureaucrat who doesn't have to worry about how he treats others.

The widow has a need—she apparently needs protection from an opponent. We aren't told why she has this need. Perhaps she is seeking to manage the estate of her deceased husband. Perhaps she is feeling the bite of predators as described by Micah and Isaiah. But regardless, she needs help and seeks it from this judge.

According to the Law of Moses, this should have taken the judge only a few minutes to decide. Exodus 22:22–24 states, "You shall not mistreat any widow or fatherless child. If you do mistreat them, and they cry out to me, I will surely hear their cry, and my wrath will burn, and I will kill you with the sword, and your wives shall become widows and your children fatherless."

God made Himself clear. You abuse and take advantage of the most vulnerable of society—the widows and orphans—and He will judge you so that your wife is a widow and your children orphans.

The judge in Jesus' parable ignored this warning, at least initially. When the widow asked for protection against her opponent, the judge turned a deaf ear. He refused to listen to her. The story does not tell us why he was so obstinate. Perhaps he didn't want to be bothered by her. Maybe he believed she would go away if he didn't give her what she needed.

But she doesn't go away. Jesus says she kept coming to him, indicating that she made a fresh appeal to the judge every day when he set up his court. The pressure never waned and the appeals never stopped. Finally, the judge gives in. He says to himself, "Though I neither fear God nor respect man, yet because this widow keeps bothering me, I will give her justice, so that she will not beat me down by her continual coming" (Luke 18:4b–5). Reluctantly—and for all the wrong reasons—he gives her a hearing. She gets what she needs, and the unjust judge gladly turns to the next case on his docket.

We read such a story and question whether a person could truly be so compassionless. Note that the parable gains no adverse reaction from the listening disciples. They knew that this was not a fictional story. Such judges existed back in the first century— as they still do today—because of a common, shared, human condition: sin. Sin darkens our understanding and hardens our hearts. It causes judges and juries to render terribly wrong decisions, as in the cases of Juan Rivera, Daniel Taylor, and many others.

THE RENEWAL OF THE MIND

Sin's pervasive effect can't be negated through our own efforts, as diligent as they may be. Jesus once said that you can clean the outside of the cup, but the inside can remain filthy (Matt. 23:25–26). Our best attempts to override the darkened mind will fail.

Our best attempts to override the darkened mind will fail.

Only the one who can break the power of sin and give us a new nature can help us start to renew our minds. When we place our trust in Christ alone as our Savior, the Holy Spirit comes to live within us, and the lifelong transformation process begins. "Do not be conformed to this world, but be transformed by the renewal of your mind, that by testing you may discern what is the will of God, what is good and acceptable and perfect" (Rom. 12:2).

If justice means applying God's moral standards to the conduct of man, "discerning the will of God" is a necessity. This insight comes progressively as believers intentionally and daily seek to renew their minds through reading and meditating on God's Word. "The law of the LORD is perfect, reviving the soul; the testimony of the LORD is sure, making wise the simple; the precepts of the LORD are right, rejoicing the heart; the commandment of the LORD is pure, enlightening the eyes" (Ps. 19:7–8).

Those who don't know Christ as their Savior have not started on that renewal journey yet. The darkened understanding still grips them. We as believers are people in process who, like Paul, are still pressing on "toward the goal for the prize of the upward call of God in Christ Jesus" (Phil. 3:14).

None of us have arrived at perfection yet. Unfortunately

this means justice remains elusive. Some of our decisions will be closer to God's righteous standard while others fall far short—not because a desire for justice is absent, but because sin has darkened our minds.

CHAPTER 6

THE NEUROLOGICAL REASON: WE HAVE IMPLICIT BIAS

The Florida jury had to render a verdict. A seventeen-year-old male had been shot and killed in an upscale, gated Sanford neighborhood by a neighborhood watch captain. The shooter, George Zimmerman, waited for police to arrive at the scene and then admitted his role in the death. That much was clear. At question was his claim that he killed in self-defense.

The African American teenager, Trayvon Martin, had walked from the home of family friends to the local convenience store to buy a bag of Skittles and a can of Arizona watermelon juice. He was wearing a hoodie. Zimmerman, aware of recent burglaries in the neighborhood, decided that Martin appeared suspicious, so he called 911. Ultimately, an altercation in the street occurred— of which the facts remain in dispute—and Zimmerman shot and killed the unarmed teenager with his .9 mm handgun.

Initially the police made no arrest. After considerable national media coverage, Zimmerman was arrested and charged with second-degree murder. The judge, Debra Nelson, demanded a color-blind trial and refused to allow any claims of racial prejudice. The state argued for conviction on an unprovoked killing. The defense claimed Zimmerman was only defending himself as allowed by Florida law.

After hearing all of the arguments and seeing all of the evidence, the twelve-person jury of local residents had to make a decision: convict or acquit. When they chose to acquit Zimmerman, the loud and demonstrative reaction was split down racial lines. The white community was mostly satisfied, believing justice had been served. The African American community was mostly outraged, convinced it hadn't.[1]

Even though the judge in the Martin case asked for a trial in which race would not be a factor, neuroscience reveals this to be an impossibility because of the reality of implicit bias.

Implicit bias is a term not often found in our vocabularies. It refers to the unconscious attitudes or stereotypes that affect our decisions and actions. Over time, on a mostly subconscious level, we learn associations. Then when we see or hear one thing, we are triggered to think of another thing previously associated with it. A common example is the sight of lightning ripping across the sky. When we see lightning we anticipate a loud crack of thunder, so we may cover our ears.

Applying the concept of subconscious associations to social relationships and decisions shows how implicit bias unconsciously affects how we think, feel, and act toward others based on race, ethnicity, or appearance. We can have a bias for them or against them without realizing it. Robustly supported by scientific research, here are some of the characteristics of implicit bias:

Implicit bias differs from explicit bias.

Explicit bias includes prejudice known to us and evident in our speech, opinions, and actions. We can be aware of prejudice we harbor toward a person, group, or race because it is voluntary and intentional. Implicit bias is different; it is unconscious, involuntary, and unintentional. It is the result of subconscious associations our brain makes based on experiences we have had starting at a very young age, including exposure to media or news programming. While we can and do have implicit attitudes toward particular kinds of food or political values, research shows that the most striking implicit bias is toward members of stigmatized groups, such as African Americans.

Implicit bias is in all of us.

While we would like to consider ourselves unbiased in our judgments, we aren't. Implicit bias is pervasive. We all have the same wiring structure in our brains, and we all have the same struggles with true impartiality. This is even true of judges who make an avowed commitment to objectivity.

While we would like to consider ourselves unbiased in our judgments, we aren't.

Implicit bias generally favors our in-group, but there are exceptions.

Our in-group is the group we are born into, associate with, or are externally identified with. I am a white male raised in the Midwest. That is my in-group. Research shows that most people have a bias toward their in-group and against those who are not in their in-group. But studies also show that people can have an implicit bias against those in their own in-group. As an example, some African Americans have demonstrated a bias against other blacks and are in favor of Caucasians.

Columnist David Brooks once wrote concerning the research, "Both blacks and whites subtly try to get a white partner when asked to team up to do an intellectually difficult task. In computer shooting simulations, both black and white participants were more likely to think black figures were armed."[2]

Implicit bias is morally neutral, not intrinsically sinful.

Our brains make associations automatically; it's what we do with those associations that has a moral quality.

God made our brains to create a constant stream of associations based on our past experiences. This helps us to process, evaluate, and make judgments. Some of these implicit, unconscious signals are positive, such as avoiding fire after being burned. Some are negative, such as linking certain groups with violence or crime. Our brains make associations automatically; it's what we do with those associations that has a moral quality.

SOCIETAL EVIDENCE OF IMPLICIT BIAS

The research on implicit bias is moving forward at an accelerated pace. MIT professor Dr. Nancy Hopkins captured the significance of studying implicit bias in her 2014 Commencement Baccalaureate Address at Boston University: "If you asked me to name the greatest discoveries on the past 50 years, alongside things like the internet and the Higgs particle, I would include the discovery of unconscious biases and the extent to which stereotypes . . . deprive people of equal opportunity in the workplace and equal justice in society."[3] The Kirwan Institute of Ohio State University publishes an annual review of this research,[4] showing how implicit bias affects decisions throughout our society.

Health Care

Repeated studies reveal uneven health care for different racial groups. Proportionately, Asian Americans die of cancer more than any other ethnic group. Yet as a group they are the least likely to be recommended for cancer screenings.[5] When doctors were shown patient histories and asked to make judgments about heart disease, they were much less likely to recommend cardiac catheterization to black patients—even when the patients' medical files were statistically identical to those of white patients.[6]

Education

Bias has a major impact on the classroom. More African American students—especially African American boys—receive more out-of-school suspensions and expulsions than white students.[7] In Portland, African American students are nearly five times as likely to be expelled or suspended than white students.[8]

Housing

Bias affects a person's ability to find and secure suitable housing. A regularly repeated study by the federal Department of Housing and Urban Development sent African Americans and whites to look at apartments, finding that African Americans were shown fewer apartments to rent and fewer houses for sale.[9] This caused two researchers to report, "Whatever the underlying causes of implicit bias may prove to be, its existence provides an

additional layer of insight into why housing inequality and segregation persist despite the dismantling of an express racial order
in American property law."[10] In other words, regardless of what's
causing implicit bias, it is displayed even in the housing market.

Employment

According to the Kirwan Institute, implicit bias flourishes in
the workplace. Research shows that a résumé with a prototypically African American–sounding name must be submitted to
50 percent more companies than the exact same résumé with a
prototypically white-sounding name.[11] Favoritism toward the
in-group typically brings candidates similar to people already in
the company.[12]

JUSTICE AND IMPLICIT BIAS

Implicit bias affects nearly every aspect of our judicial system.
Law professor Adam Benforado says it like this:

> Even if we quashed all the familiar problems that can derail
> a case, even if our system operated exactly as it was designed
> to, we would still end up with wrongful convictions, biased
> proceedings, trampled rights, and unequal treatment. Injus-
> tice is built into our legal structures and influences outcomes
> every minute of every day. And its origins lie not inside the
> dark heart of a bigoted police officer or a scheming D. A. but
> within the mind of each and every one of us.[13]

Since everyone in the system—from the police on the streets
to the judges and juries in the courtroom—has a measure of
implicit, unconscious bias, true justice remains elusive.

Shooter Bias

Police officers must make split-second decisions—often to save their own lives and the lives of others. With just a few clues processed in a flash, they have to decide, "Do I shoot, or not?" Recognizing this daily dilemma, research shows an implicit bias toward those who are shot.

A 2015 *Washington Post* study showed police in the previous year had shot and killed a disproportionate number of unarmed, African American men.[14] The 990 documented fatal shootings revealed unarmed black men were seven times more likely to die from police gunfire than unarmed white men. When adjusted for other variables such as age, mental illness, and the crime rate of the neighborhood, the key factor in predicting if an unarmed person would be shot was his skin color.

There is no evidence that the black individuals were attacking the police officers. In fact, the study showed that they were less likely to attack than white individuals. "This just bolsters our confidence that there is some sort of implicit bias going on. Officers are perceiving a greater threat when encountered by unarmed black citizens."[15]

A trio of legal scholars explains that this way:

Black citizens are often associated with violence, dangerousness, and crime. The process might go something like this. A person sees a black face. The brain categorizes the person as being black, which in turn triggers a storehouse of beliefs about black people: they are dangerous, criminal, violent. Without consciously comparing the automatically-activated, stereotype-driven knowledge to consciously held ethical beliefs or to careful fact checking, the brain uses this stereotypic knowledge as a filter through which other incoming information is processed.[16]

Tragically, that processing often leads to a gun being fired.

Bias on the Bench

Judges vow to maintain impartiality in their courtrooms. But with unconscious associations running through their brains, they also fall victim to implicit bias. In one study noted by the Kirwan Institute in their 2013 review, researchers showed that 87.1 percent of white judges in the study displayed a strong preference toward white people.[17] This unconscious preference makes it difficult—even impossible—for judges to remain objective, even though they clearly believe they are neutral. When one researcher asked a group of judges to rank their ability to remain free of racial prejudice in their decisions, a stunning 97 percent believed they should be ranked in the top 50 percent.[18] Not only is this a statistical impossibility, but a perception of objectivity can actually foster more biased decisions.

Bias among Jurors

Jurors, like judges, take a pledge of objectivity when they agree to serve. While they are intent on fulfilling this commitment, the job of a juror is deeply affected by implicit bias because of the nature of their task. Jurors are given instructions by the judge and are asked to consider the evidence set forth in the trial. Based on this, they are to render a verdict.

As I mentioned in chapter four, we never have all the facts. We discover as many pertinent facts as possible to build a case, but ultimately the minds of the jury must connect the dots and complete the picture. Inevitably, though, their subconscious biases will color the narrative, both as it unfolds in the court and forms in their mind. One researcher says, "When serving on a jury, jurors are required to connect details from a trial and often rely on schemas to fill in the narrative gaps. This strategy can make jury members particularly vulnerable to the effects of implicit bias."[19]

A lawyer lamented this reality as she considered the jury selection process. Talking about those who would populate the jury room, she said this about jurors:

> [They] come from all walks of life: they are retired school-teachers, electricians, unemployed factory workers, homemakers, and church leaders. They are young, middle-aged, and elderly. They are straight and gay, male and female, black, white, Asian and Latino. They are Good Americans. And like all of us, they harbor implicit biases about people of different races, ethnicities, and genders. Can a jury rife with implicit biases fulfill its role as a bulwark of liberty and an "anchor to the principles of the Constitution"?[20]

Simply put, even our juries—which are put in place for the sole purpose of bolstering objectivity—cannot escape implicit bias.

Bias in Sentencing

Implicit bias is evident in sentencing more than in any other part of the judicial process. We knowingly or unknowingly show bias based on others' skin color, education, gender, or socioeconomic status. This is illustrated in the disparate tales of two Texas teenagers who committed intoxication manslaughter.

Jaime Arellano crossed the US–Mexico border illegally with his family as a teenager. Settled in East Texas, once he learned to drive he ignored his parents' warnings and occasionally drove under the influence. This often ends in tragedy, and in this case it did. At age sixteen, on June 23, 2007, Arellano was driving an SUV with an open beer in his hand when he swerved wildly in an intersection and rammed into a Ford Mustang that was making a left turn. The driver of the car, a thirty-one-year-old mother who was nine months pregnant with her second child, was killed. Her unborn child also perished.

Moved to the adult court, Arellano had two options presented to him by the prosecution: accept a plea deal with a promise of twenty years in prison and possible parole after ten years, or face a jury trial with conviction bringing a maximum of fifty years in prison. He pled guilty and started serving his time in Huntsville, Texas. He becomes eligible for parole in 2017 and, if he gains parole, expects to be immediately deported to Mexico.[21]

A much different scenario unfolded for a second Texas teenager. Ethan Couch was sixteen years old on the night of June 15, 2013. He drove his red pickup from a party at the second home of his parents—with triple the legal limit of alcohol in his blood. Seven friends were in the truck with him. As Couch recklessly drove down the country road at almost seventy miles per hour—even playing chicken with oncoming cars—he slammed into a crowd of people surrounding a disabled SUV. The stranded motorist—a youth pastor—and a mother with her daughter were all killed in the crash. Two others were serious injured.

Couch, a Caucasian from a wealthy family, was charged with the same counts as Arellano: intoxication manslaughter and intoxication assault. However, with a high-powered legal team at his side, the case was moved into juvenile court. When convicted, the prosecutors argued for a twenty-year sentence—the same as Arellano. The judge decided that Couch wouldn't serve jail time and sentenced him to ten years of probation. Along with the probation was a requirement to enter rehab treatment.

Two Texas teenagers. Two horrific accidents from driving under the influence. Identical charges. Completely different outcomes. A poor Hispanic boy gets twenty years. A rich white boy gets probation.[22] This is partiality in all its ungodly splendor.

This is partiality in all its ungodly splendor.

Bias Statistics

Minority residents of Chicago know exactly what this means. They regularly experience bias and partiality from the police force. According to the lengthy report of the city-authorized Police Accountability Task Force,[23] people of color—especially African Americans—are disproportionately stopped, tasered, shot, and killed by Chicago police. In a city roughly divided into thirds between whites, African Americans, and Hispanics, the statistics are startling:

- Of 404 police shootings between 2008–2015, 74 percent of those shot were African American, 14 percent were Hispanic, and 8 percent were white.
- Of 1,886 police Taser discharges between 2012–2015, 76 percent of those tasered were African American, 13 percent were Hispanic, and 8 percent were white.
- Of the more than 250,000 traffic stops by police in the summer of 2014, 72 percent involved African Americans, 17 percent involved Hispanics, and 9 percent involved whites. Black and Hispanic drivers

were searched four times as often as white drivers, even though police data reveals contraband was found twice as often on white drivers than on blacks or Hispanics.

- In a 2015 survey of twelve hundred Chicago residents over the age of sixteen, an estimated 70 percent of the young African American males reported being stopped by police in the previous twelve months.[24]

Research shows bias is equally evident in capital punishment cases. In more than two thousand Georgia murder cases, defendants who killed a white person were sentenced to death 11 percent of the time, while defendants who killed a black person were sentenced to death only 1 percent of the time. Conversely, a black person who killed a white person was twenty-two times more likely to receive the death penalty than a white person who killed a black person.[25]

A similar study in North Carolina—a study of 15,000 homicides over more than twenty-five years—revealed that a defendant was three times more likely to receive the death penalty for killing a white person than a black person.[26] In Louisiana, a study of 1,100 capital crimes between 1990–2008 showed that prosecutors pursued the death penalty 364 percent more often when the victim was white.[27] The conclusions are inescapable. "The bottom line is that black individuals do worse as both defendants and victims in capital trials." [28]

The death penalty, as stated by the US Supreme Court, is reserved for the worst offenders who commit the worst crimes. How is that determined? The introduction of (1) aggravating factors, which seek to show the heinous quality of the crime and why it is deserving of death, and (2) mitigating factors, which seek to show reasons why a life sentence is more appropriate. The jurors are asked to balance these factors and determine the right sentence for the crime. This leaves plenty of room for implicit bias.

Researchers cite two factors that are shown to trigger jurors' implicit bias. The first is when prosecutors *dehumanize the defendant*, or suggest that the defendant is less than human, like an animal that should be kept in a cage. Studies have clearly shown that when the accused is described in subhuman terms, the jurors pronounce harsher sentences[29] because they are not prescribing the death of another human, but of something less than human.

The second trigger for implicit bias, which is used to bring mitigating evidence to the table, is *having jurors empathetically identify with the defendant's position.* Since most jurors in capital cases are white, this is more easily accomplished if the defendant is white; it is more challenging if the defendant is black. The jurors can often more easily place themselves in the shoes of a white defendant. They lack empathy for an African American, especially if the defendant is described in dehumanizing terms during the trial.[30]

Two researchers make this disheartening conclusion: "Ultimately, the decision to sentence a person to death is based not on a rational determination, a weighing of the evidence, or the finding that the particular defendant is indeed guilty of the worst of the worst offenses, but rather on a series of unconscious decisions, by prosecutors, judges, jurors, and even defense lawyers in which race affects the processing of the underlying evidence and tilts the scales of justice."[31] Adam Benforado adds, "It's not just whether you are black; it's how black you are. The broadness of a defendant's nose, the thickness of his lips, and the darkness of his skin have all been correlated with capital punishment decisions."[32]

This is not just. This is not equality. But this is the reality of implicit bias. Until the role unconscious bias plays in a capital murder trial—and all sentences—is recognized, and intentional steps are taken to limit the influence of a jury's bias, the scales will remain sadly tipped. Supreme Court Justice Harry Blackmun, in a 1994 dissenting opinion, said, "Even under the most sophisticated of death penalty statutes, race continues to play a major role in determining who shall live and who shall die."[33]

EVIDENCE OF PROGRESS

I am encouraged when I read about a growing number of police associations, judges, and attorneys who are seeking training to better understand their biases—and work towards counteracting them. Some of these initiatives include:

- *Implicit bias testing.* Faculty at Harvard University have developed an instrument to help this training process called the Implicit Association Test (IAT).[34] This test measures attitudes and beliefs we may be either unwilling to report or unable to recognize. It also uses a reaction-time measure to evaluate the strength of associations already existing in our brain to help us build awareness of our subconscious biases.
- *Law enforcement initiatives.* Many police departments are already taking steps to combat implicit bias by offering training for their officers and utilizing body cameras in an effort to increase transparency and build trust.
- *Mandatory federal training.* Recently the US Justice Department announced mandatory training for its 33,000 federal agents and prosecutors to help prevent implicit bias from influencing law-enforcement

decisions.[35] This move on the federal level was in response to encouraging results of training in unconscious biases conducted on the local level.

• *Jury awareness.* Alert judges are seeking to counteract this bias vulnerability by making juries aware of how stereotypes and racial images can affect their decision making.[36] Therefore, instead of pursuing a colorblind trial, as proposed in the Zimmerman trial in Florida, the better approach is to make race salient.

In the last three chapters, we've examined three inescapable reasons justice remains elusive. We cannot change some realities of life, including our limited knowledge, darkened understanding, and implicit bias. But these challenges do not negate our responsibility to pursue justice. In the next chapters we will dig into practical things we can change and actions we can take.

PART 3

HOW SHOULD
WE DO JUSTICE?

CHAPTER 7

THE ENDURING DIVINE REQUIREMENT

My beloved car had a problem. In fact, it had a *major* problem. Every morning the driveway at my parents' house received a fresh deposit of red fluid relentlessly dripping from the transmission of my 1964 Oldsmobile Dynamic 88. A closer inspection revealed the seals were leaking—badly.

I was a poor college student. The little cash I had in my savings account was dutifully earmarked for tuition, not for transmission repair. I tried to outwit the problem by refilling the reservoir with fresh transmission fluid every day. As long as I just took the car on short jaunts around town, I could—barely—keep enough fluid in the transmission to keep the gears from slipping. But the leak soon resembled a crimson Niagara Falls, and I knew that I had no choice. If I wanted the car to run, I had to fix the seals myself.

I was, and still am, far from a gearhead. Fortunately my dad came armed with his vast assortment of tools and the know-how for tackling a project like this, and he climbed under the car with me. With the chassis of the car just inches above our heads, we started disconnecting the transmission from the drive shaft. Two rusty bolts and three bloody knuckles later, I started throwing tools around and complaining, "This is hard! I don't want to do this!"

My dad is a patient man, and he listened to my whining for a while. Finally his patience expired and he said, "Just because something is difficult doesn't mean it can't or shouldn't be done. If you want to use your car, you have to do what is necessary to get it running again. Otherwise, park it and walk!"

In my mind, walking was not an option. So I kept laboring—skinned knuckles and all—on the challenging task before me.

WHAT GOD REQUIRES

In chapter 6 of his prophecy, Micah uses a courtroom motif to press God's case against the rebellious Israelites. God, through His prophet, is the prosecuting attorney. Israel sits conspicuously alone at the defense table. The trial begins in verse 2 with Micah inviting the very mountains to listen: "Hear, you mountains, the indictment of the LORD, and you enduring foundations of the earth, for the LORD has an indictment against his people, and he will contend with Israel."

What is the charge God brings against his people? Infidelity. Much like an attorney pleading a client's case, Micah speaks on behalf of God, saying:

> O my people, what have I done to you? How have I wearied you? Answer me! For I brought you up from the land of Egypt and redeemed you from the house of slavery, and I sent before you Moses, Aaron, and Miriam. O my people, remember what Balak king of Moab devised, and what Balaam the son of Beor answered him, and what happened from Shittim to Gilgal, that you may know the righteous acts of the LORD. (Micah 6:3–5)

God accuses His people of not rightly responding to the love and kindness He showed them. He gives repeated evidence of how He acted graciously on their behalf—providing deliverance from slavery and exceptional leaders—but He implies that He received insufficient devotion in return.

The courtroom drama suddenly shifts in verse 6, with the defense offering its response to the charges. Israel asks God what he might expect from them. "With what shall I come before the LORD, and bow myself before God on high? Shall I come before Him with burnt offerings, with calves a year old? Will the LORD be pleased with thousands of rams, with ten thousands of rivers of oil? Shall I give my firstborn for my transgression, the fruit of my body for the sin of my soul?" (vv. 6–7).

Israel's people claim that they will bring God anything that He desires in return for His grace. Nothing is too much to consider, even extremely costly gifts. The nation is willing to bring thousands of burnt offerings, tens of thousands of oil offerings—even the unspeakable sacrifice of their firstborn children. The implication clearly is, "you name it, we'll do it." Then the defense attorney sits down with a smug look on his face.

The heavenly cameras shift back to the prosecuting attorney for his response. What does God want from His people for all His kindnesses to them? Micah explains that God has already made His demands clear. "He has told you, O man, what is good; and what does the LORD require of you but to do justice, and to love kindness, and to walk humbly with your God?" (v. 8).

> **Do justice, and love kindness, and walk humbly with your God.**

It is stated as a question, but no verbal response is expected.

What does God require of His people, whom He loves? Not a mountain of sacrificed rams. Not a river of oil. Especially not the brutal murder of their children. They may claim ignorance, but God has told them what is good and what He requires: godly, ethical behavior, which is summarized in three simple phrases.

Do justice.

Love kindness.

Walk humbly.

While the last two phrases are vital to our walk as believers and must not be ignored, the first phrase is riveting and our focus in this book. *Do justice.* Do what is right and just in the eyes of the Lord.

NO EXCUSES

Yes, justice is elusive because of our limited knowledge, darkened understanding, and implicit bias. It may be difficult to get right all the time due to our creaturely confines. God understands this; He's our maker. But He doesn't stutter here. Despite our limitations and propensity to sin, He still requires that we *do justice.*

We must do what's right in our interactions with others because God created us all in His image. No excuses. No complaints that it's too difficult. With every ounce of energy, with unyielding focus, and with unbridled passion, we are to pursue justice.

Our humanity will inevitably limit our success. It's like drawing a straight line. In the early classes of my architectural training I received instruction on basic drawing skills, including the proper way to print letters and draw a straight line. Believe it or not, drawing a straight line across a piece of paper takes skill. Some can do it better than others. Yet no one—not even the most skilled architect on the planet—can draw a perfectly straight line. The best effort will always be imperfect.

The same is true in our attempts to do justice. But now that we've surveyed the challenges, it's time to focus on the positives. The options and possibilities for how we can do justice are limited only by our imagination and willingness. Let's explore some of the political, public, and personal ways we can live out God's command to *do justice.*

CHAPTER 8

DOING JUSTICE IN THE POLITICAL ARENA

It was election day. Living in downtown Chicago—where we walk more than we drive—I made my way through the streets to the community center where my precinct voted. A small collection of colorful candidate signs marked the entrance. Unfamiliar with the building, I finally navigated my way to the correct room and walked in, expecting it to be bustling with activity and energy.

A morgue would have looked more alive.

Several civic-minded volunteers sat behind tables laden with thick registers of voters. I looked to see to which person I was to report to, as last names were divided according to the alphabet. But it wouldn't have made any difference. Lines were not a problem that morning. I was the only voter in the room. I was significantly outnumbered by the volunteers!

I was handed my ballot, given my instructions, and directed to use any empty voting booth. I had my choice. They were *all* empty.

Feeling like everyone in the room was watching me complete my ballot, I marked my choices and walked over to the pleasant gentleman manning the electronic ballot box. He gave me guidance for the proper insertion of my ballot into the hungry machine, and I fed my paper into its mouth. It gobbled my votes up like a hungry teenager, and a red digital number danced on the screen: 33. I stared at it for a brief moment before realizing the sad reality. I live in Chicago along with a couple million other registered voters. I had walked into the polling place at a prime time in the morning, and not only was it deserted of other voters, but I was only the thirty-third person to cast a ballot. Mountains of names in the voter registers, but only thirty-two voters before me. As I left the room I saw no one behind me. I wondered when voter thirty-four would show up.

THE GOVERNMENT AND JUSTICE

Our concern in this book is for justice. As I've shown, justice is not necessarily defined by what is legal in our land; laws are just only as far as they align with biblical standards. To explore the practical ways we can do justice, we must start in the political arena.

No institution has a greater role in the execution of justice, or the lack of it, than the government. As I mentioned in chapter 2, this is God's design. He gave governments the authority to execute justice. "Whoever resists the authorities resists what God has appointed, and those who resist will incur judgment. For rulers are not a terror to good conduct, but to bad" (Rom. 13:2–3).

The Preamble to our nation's Constitution clearly recognizes our government's role in the establishment of justice. It says that government should "establish Justice, insure domestic Tranquility, provide for the common defense, promote the general Welfare, and secure the Blessings of Liberty to ourselves and our Posterity."[1]

Note what appears first in the list of obligations for the government: establish justice. As a republic with democratic representation, our government seeks to establish justice by passing laws through the legislative branch and interpreting those laws through the judicial branch. Citizens participate in the process—and thereby the establishment of justice—through the election of the president, senators, representatives, governors, mayors, and, in certain cases, judges.

> **Though we may withhold our vote, we cannot neglect our responsibility to do justice.**

Though we may withhold our vote, we cannot neglect our responsibility to do justice. That remains. By not voting, we severely mute any influence we may have had on our government's right execution of justice.

This is the troubling part of the thirty-three voters at my deserted polling station. And while it may not represent every precinct, it is illustrative of a true problem. When Christian voters choose not to cast a ballot, they forfeit an opportunity to exert "significant influence."[2] A key way to hold government accountable disappears. Lacking this accountability, and void of a moral compass, the government inevitably degenerates. Respected theologian Wayne Grudem urges Christians to vote when he asks, "If Christians do not speak publicly about moral and ethical issues facing a nation, who will? Where will people learn about ethics? Where will a nation learn how to tell right from wrong?"[3]

The answer is clear: nowhere. The blind lead the blind, and the outcome—reflecting the wickedness of the human heart—is rarely a reflection of biblical justice. Stephen Monsma, senior research fellow at the Henry Institute for the Study of Christianity and Politics, paints an even starker picture:

> Government—that institution God has equipped to be a powerful means to redress wrongs and establish justice—has

a tremendous potential for evil. Human society already has a tendency to produce evil structures in which the powerful oppress the poor and vulnerable, and government is meant to fight such structures. But government itself can all too easily become an evil structure.[4]

Human government can slide into such an evil structure because of constant cultural change. The cultural change cycle starts when society encounters a new idea and champions emerge to promote this new value.[5] A debate ensues (sometimes formal, often informal), and the nation determines if it will adopt the idea—think the acceptance of same-sex marriage—into the culture.

Once a law is passed, the tipping point has been reached. All that remains is the full integration of the value into the culture. The time to biblically evaluate and perhaps contest an idea is earlier in the process, when we vote. By casting a ballot for a candidate, we seek to influence the nation by placing someone into office who supports biblical justice and is concerned about what God is concerned about.

GOD'S CONCERNS

While cultural concerns morph in different directions over time, God's concerns endure. Therefore, before casting a vote we should always seek to understand the candidate's stand on the following justice issues, which are not an exhaustive list but are certainly top priorities.

Individual Liberty

God created man to be free. Not autonomous—no creature is autonomous in the presence of a sovereign God—but free. Free to determine his livelihood, free to travel, free to speak openly and frankly, and especially free to worship God in a manner consistent with his conscience.

Our American forefathers recognized this in the Declaration of Independence when they wrote, "We hold these truths to be self-evident, that all men are created equal, that they are endowed by their Creator with certain unalienable Rights, that among these are Life, Liberty and the pursuit of Happiness."[6]

This was clarified in the First Amendment to the US Constitution, which states, "Congress shall make no law respecting an establishment of religion, or prohibiting the free exercise thereof; or abridging the freedom of speech, or of the press; or of the right of the people peaceably to assemble, and to petition the Government for a redress of grievances."[7]

Government leaders can suffocate individual liberty through laws designed to wrongly control its citizens. Religious liberty, despite its stated protections in the First Amendment, is clearly under attack in our society. The freedom to follow the teachings of Scripture is increasingly being classified as bigoted, discriminatory, and unlawful behavior.[8] As more believers, religious nonprofits, and Christian schools experience persecution or face lawsuits due to the loss of religious freedoms, our role in politics has great implications for justice.

It is now up to individual states to defend religious freedoms.[9] The Religious Freedom Restoration Act (RFRA) was originally passed by the federal government in 1993 to protect religious freedom, but in 1997 the Supreme Court ruled that states had to enact their own version of the RFRA if they wanted its provisions. About twenty states have done so, most recently Indiana, Mississippi, and North Carolina. Others will never even consider such legislation. Even when such a law passes, a governor can veto it, as was the case in Georgia.

This becomes an important issue to consider when voting for a candidate: what is his or her stand on individual liberty and, more specifically, religious freedom—and not just for Christianity, but for any religion?

Sanctity of Life

The murder of the unborn is a justice issue. As I noted earlier, every human life is sacred, created by God, and deserving of legal protection against termination. Since the 1973 *Roe v. Wade* decision, our nation has allowed abortion clinics to snuff out the lives of millions of souls.

While it seems popular opinion is turning more pro-life in recent years, the law will remain until struck down by the US Supreme Court. That means this issue is in the hands of the executive branch, the future presidents who will nominate Supreme Court justices, and the legislative branch, the future senators who will confirm such nominations. With a sharply divided court today, every vacancy on the bench creates an opportunity to appoint a justice inclined to overturn this unjust law.

Consider this before casting your vote. Is your candidate pro-life?

Incarceration Rates

America leads the world in putting people behind bars—and our pace is accelerating. Consider these statistics:

- Since 1970, we have seen a more than 500 percent increase in our prison population, with 2.2 million people in our jails and prisons on any given day.[10]

- We incarcerate people five to ten times more often than most other industrialized nations.[11]
- We have 5 percent of the world's population and 25 percent of its prisoners.[12]

One group of researchers offered these sobering statistics:

The size and pervasiveness of the criminal justice regime have no parallel in history. . . . If we count those individuals who are currently on probation or parole, more than 7 million men and women are under legal supervision—a number equal to the population of Israel . . . at the turn of the millennium, approximately 1.5 million children had at least one parent in jail or prison, and 10 million have had a parent in jail at some time during their lives.[13]

What accounts for this rapid rise in imprisonment? Stiffer and mandatory sentences, which have been enforced over the last twenty-five years in an effort to make streets safer. In many states with "three strikes" laws, criminals with two previous convictions can expect a mandatory life sentence if convicted a third time—even if none of the crimes were violent. We are not just incarcerating dangerous people; we are putting sizeable numbers of people in prison who have substance abuse problems and mental health issues.

These monstrous incarceration rates have a racist tinge to them. Adam Benforado gives this chilling

"A country that abolished slavery 150 years ago now has a greater number of black men in the correctional system than there were slaves in 1850 . . ."

observation: "A country that abolished slavery 150 years ago now has a greater number of black men in the correctional system than there were slaves in 1850, and a greater percentage of its black population in jail than was imprisoned in apartheid South Africa. Black, male, and no high school diploma? It's more likely than not that you will spend time in prison during your life."[14]

I have the high privilege of serving on the Board of Directors for the National Association of Evangelicals (NAE). More than thirty years ago, well before my service on the board started, the NAE adopted a resolution calling for sentencing reform. It said, "Dangerous criminals must be imprisoned to protect society. However, half of those in prison have been convicted of nonviolent offenses. As an alternative or supplement to incarceration, biblically-based sanctions, such as restitution, would benefit the victim of the crime and society in general, as well as help to rehabilitate the offender. Incidentally, the cost of this approach would be only a fraction of incarceration."[15]

This is a sound, biblical approach to the pressing problem of incarceration today, but it is not popular among politicians who want to avoid any appearance of being "soft on crime." Reelection bids usually run on the candidate's promise to bite down on crime. But our mass incarceration policy is not working, and it is rapidly becoming untenable financially. Other approaches must be explored. Recently Texas, famous for its tough stance on crime, explored ways to reverse its exploding inmate growth population, with encouraging results.[16]

Before you vote, consider the views of your candidate on this justice issue. Where would he or she stand on incarceration?

Societal Safety Net

God is concerned for the most vulnerable of society. When

He gave the Law to the nation of Israel, He emphasized the just treatment of widows, orphans, strangers, and the poor. Nicholas Wolterstorff called these "the quartet of the vulnerable."[17] God commanded the Israelites to protect them, saying,

> You shall not wrong a sojourner, or oppress him, for you were sojourners in the land of Egypt. You shall not mistreat any widow or fatherless child. If you do mistreat them, and they cry out to me, I will surely hear their cry, and my wrath will burn . . . If you lend money to any of my people with you who is poor, you shall not be like a moneylender to him, and you shall not exact interest from him. If ever you take your neighbor's cloak in pledge, you shall return it to him before the sun goes down, for that is his only covering, and it is his cloak for his body; in what else shall he sleep? And if he cries to me, I will hear, for I am compassionate. (Ex. 22:21–27)

I will discuss our personal responsibility to the most vulnerable of society in the next chapters, but here the issue is the role of government in creating and maintaining an adequate safety net. This is a justice issue to God. Rulers, leaders, and judges have a responsibility before God to take up the cause of the poor, for usually those on the bottom shelves of society suffer the most. In our country, the fastest growing segment of the poor

God is concerned for the most vulnerable of society.

are children.[18] Across our land, despite our wealth, 20 percent of our children live below the poverty line—struggling to gain adequate nutrition, health care, housing, and schooling.[19] We tend to blame the poor for their poverty. Children cannot be blamed for

We tend to blame the poor for their poverty. Children cannot be blamed for their poverty. They just need help.

their poverty. They just need help.

Faith-based organizations have traditionally taken the lead in such efforts, but our government cannot ignore broader structures and systems that punish the most vulnerable among us. It's a justice issue. Does your candidate understand poverty issues? Will he or she work to strengthen the safety net that still contains too many holes?

A SIMPLE PROCESS

In the helter-skelter pace of our lives, we can easily park the important for the sake of the urgent. The urgent: sick child at home, car needing repairs, extra project from work, and flooding in the basement. Participating wisely and influentially in the political process by supporting justice through our vote does not qualify as urgent. But it is immensely important.

Many Christians fail to bring "significant influence" to the voting booth because of a lack of process. They don't have a plan to determine how they should vote, and—if they vote at all—they arrive with little preparation.[20] To that end, I offer this simple, four-step process as a guide.

Know the issues.

The issues change as society changes. Traditional marriage and religious freedom were not debated three decades ago. They are huge issues today. Earlier in this chapter I listed the most significant issues we currently face. But they will change. Culture will continue to evolve and devolve, and new questions will emerge for followers of Jesus. So, to vote well we need to first identify and know what issues are important to God, such as those discussed above.

Research the candidates' positions on the issues.

This is where it can get messy—and time consuming. Unfortunately, sometimes candidates can be gloriously vague on their positions in an effort to be elected. Often they can appear to flip-flop faster than a fish in a boat. We are not omniscient and we can't know what is really in the hearts and minds of the candidates. But to the best of our ability we need to come to conclusions on where the candidates stand on the issues important to God.

Evaluate the alignment of the candidates on the issues.

We know what God wants from our study of the Word. We know what the candidates believe from our research of their positions. Now we have to determine how well they align with biblical justice. It would be rare to find a candidate who perfectly matches what God wants in a leader or judge. But choose the candidate you think gets closest.

Pray for those who are elected.

No matter who wins an election, our obligation as Christians remains. God calls us to regularly intercede for our leaders. Paul commands us, "I urge that supplications, prayers, intercessions, and thanksgivings be made for all people, for kings and all who are in high positions, that we may lead a peaceful and quiet life, godly and dignified in every way" (1 Tim. 2:1–2). The implication is clear: prayers for our leaders, that they may cultivate an environment conducive to godly living and the spread of the gospel. We must not stumble here. I often wonder if a lack of prayer for our leaders is a main reason for the downward spiral of our society. Let's vote—and then get on our knees.

This is doing justice in the political arena. In our country, we can influence who is elected and promote biblical justice. As R. C. Sproul once wrote, "With every vote and every law and every behavioral choice, we must ask the question, Is it right?"[21]

CHAPTER 9

DOING JUSTICE
IN THE PUBLIC ARENA

Sixteen-year-old Kalief Browder spent three years locked up in the notorious Robert N. Davoren Center for juveniles, awaiting a trial that never came. He was stopped by police in May of 2010 as he walked home from a party with a friend. Browder was accused of stealing a backpack. Taken to the precinct for questioning, he remained in custody, his family unable to post bond, for over 1,000 days, waiting for his day in court to prove his innocence.

It never came.

Through a startling sequence of events involving an inexplicable string of delays by the prosecution, Browder stood before eight different judges over the three-year period. Despite the assurance from the Sixth Amendment, which promises "a speedy trial," he was never tried for the alleged crime. He just remained in custody—often in solitary confinement. As his former classmates received their high school diplomas, Browder was left to navigate daily the violent surroundings of the juvenile prison. Smallish in size and nicknamed "Peanut" by his family, he twice sought to commit suicide.

He gained release in June of 2013 when, quite suddenly, the prosecutors dropped all charges. The lone witness against Browder

"I'm not alright ... I'm messed up ... I'm mentally scarred right now ... There are certain things that changed about me and they might not go back."

had returned to his native Mexico. With no other evidence, the charges were dropped, and Browder gained his freedom.

But the marks of his wrongful incarceration have been deeply etched in his life. He told reporters, "I'm not all right.... I'm messed up.... I'm mentally scarred right now.... There are certain things that changed about me and they might not go back."[1] Reflecting on what he experienced, he said, "Before I went to jail, I didn't know a lot of stuff, and, now that I am aware, I'm paranoid. I feel like I was robbed of my happiness."[2]

Two years after his release from prison, Browder committed suicide.[3]

WHAT CAN WE DO?

Injustice happens. As painful as that reality is, justice will often remain elusive for us in this fallen world. Lives like Kalief Browder's will never be the same. But as representatives of God, we can't quit. We can't ever give up the pursuit of justice, even if our results are imperfect.

In our communities, in our nation, and in our world, how do we do that? How would God have us do justice in the public arena?

ADVOCATE FOR JUDICIAL REFORM

The United States may have the finest judicial system in the world today, but as we have seen in earlier chapters, it remains broken in key areas and is in desperate need of reform. Change can only come through political leaders, making advocacy—like calling, meeting, emailing, or signing petitions—critical in many areas, including the following.

Pretrial Limbo

Our legal system requires the posting of bail—or bond money—for a person under arrest to remain free. Bail is insurance that the person will appear for trial and not flee the legal system. But since the majority of those arrested are minorities and disproportionately poor, bail often remains beyond their grasp. They are left in pretrial limbo: innocent but in jail, unable to work, separated from family and support systems, and vulnerable to other inmates. This deepens the poverty cycle. Earlier I told the story of Kalief Browder. He is not alone. On any given day in this country, there are 476,000 pretrial detainees.[4]

Overcriminalization

In an effort to make our communities safer, more acts are being criminalized—that is, lawmakers are declaring criminal intent in more misdemeanors than before. Certainly laws are needed against violent crime, but the endless maze of regulations place unknowing citizens in jeopardy of prosecution. In Maryland the county inspector slapped a $500 fine on a half-dozen ten-year-old children for running a lemonade stand without a permit.[5] A man in Oregon who collected rain and snow runoff on his property was sentenced to thirty days in jail.[6] The increase in sanctions not only threatens our freedom but also adds to the overcrowded prisons and jails.

Proportionate Sentencing

In the past few decades, state and federal legislators have required more and harsher sentences for criminals.[7] This "get tough on crime" approach not only removed discretion from judges but also rapidly raised incarceration rates around the country, as noted earlier. Determinate sentences had good intentions, but not always good outcomes. Nonviolent crimes such as drug dealing are treated with the same recourses as murder, rape, and assault.

Another example: a financially desperate single mother with no prior criminal record was paid $100 by a complete stranger to mail a package that—unbeknownst to her—contained 200 grams of crack cocaine. She was arrested, convicted, and sentenced to ten years in prison because the judge had no freedom to be more lenient.[8] Federal lawmakers have considered relaxing mandatory minimum sentences but have not yet passed the necessary legislation.

Prison Rape

According to Bureau of Justice statistics, 80,000 incarcerated men and women are raped every year by other inmates and prison guards. This is just the number of reported incidents, which is likely massively underreported. A *New York Times* article calls prison rape America's most "open secret."[9] Juveniles and more slightly built inmates unable to protect themselves are often targeted for abuse. The refusal to acknowledge and address the problem has far-reaching and long-lasting consequences for our society, as abused ex-convicts reenter life outside the prison walls with deep psychological scars. The Prison Rape Elimination Act of 2003 requires the reporting of sexual violence, but it has done little to curb it.

Restoration of Civil Rights

When ex-cons reenter society, they are not just stepping into a strange, new world void of structure and clanging prison doors. They are also facing a life void of normal civil rights. With a felony on their record, they find employers unwilling to hire them. They encounter housing restrictions. They lack the right to vote. They usually are restricted from civic involvement. Nationwide, one in every thirteen black adults cannot vote because of a felony conviction.[10]

These realities marginalize and stigmatize an offender and prove to be significant—often insurmountable—hurdles to successful reentry. Some consequences may be necessary for an offender based upon the crime committed. But restrictions bearing no relationship to the crime unduly burden a person who has paid their penalty. These merit a careful review and potential reform.

All of these areas needing reform provide opportunities for us to practice advocacy through:

- Calling mayors, governors, state senators, congressmen, and US senators who have the ability and authority to enact judicial reform.
- Meeting with like-minded individuals to learn about the latest developments in judicial reform and what still needs to be accomplished.
- Emailing political authorities in support of pending state and federal legislation that would bring needed reform.
- Signing petitions to encourage lawmakers to consider additional judicial reform. For the latest petitions, visit the websites listed in the resources section at the back of the book.

ADVOCATE FOR THE INNOCENT

The wrongly incarcerated need an advocate. They need someone standing up for them. They need a person committed to justice who selflessly invests time pleading their cases. You do not need to be a lawyer, judge, or law enforcement officer. You just need to have a passion to see those wrongly accused gain justice.

Like Susan Carlson. Carlson started her career behind a camera. She launched a photography business in the late 1970s, identifying suitable houses in the northern suburbs of Chicago to be used for media projects. Because of her skill with a camera, in the late 1990s Carlson began to help a private investigator on projects and eventually started her own shop called Carlson Investigations.

Often using costumes and disguises as she went undercover in her research, she discovered the case of Eddie Bolden. Bolden had been sentenced to life in prison without parole after his conviction in 1996 by a county jury on two counts of murder and one count of attempted murder. Yet his conviction primarily hung on the testimony of a single dubious witness.

The murders occurred on the night of January 29, 1994. Three twentysomething men—including two brothers—drove three separate cars to the parking lot of a fish restaurant around 8 p.m. to complete a drug deal. Bolden was inside the restaurant playing a video game. The drug deal went bad and two of the men, Derrick Frazier and Irving Clayton, were shot multiple times and killed. The remaining man, Clifford Frazier, was wounded but survived.

During the police investigation, Frazier described the shooter as between 5 feet 10 inches and 6 feet tall and clean-shaven, with a medium build, light complexion, and short hair. Bolden was 6 feet 2 inches tall, very thin, bald, with a dark complexion and a mustache. It hardly seemed like a match.

Bolden came to the police station with his attorney to be placed in a lineup. Before the lineup, detectives led Frazier past Bolden, and they exchanged glances. Later, during the lineup, Frazier first identified someone else as the shooter. Given a second chance, he pegged Bolden. Based on this identification, Bolden stood trial in 1996. His defense attorney called two witnesses who testified that Bolden was inside the restaurant at the time of the shootings, but their testimony was largely ignored. He was convicted and sentenced, never expecting to see freedom again.

In her acquaintance with the case, Susan Carlson became convinced of Bolden's innocence. With painstaking work she unearthed three witnesses who were in the fish restaurant the night of the murders and would testify that Bolden was indeed inside playing a video game. None had ever been called or contacted for the trial. With these new witnesses, Carlson tirelessly hunted for an attorney to take on the case. After many unsuccessful tries, she finally found Ronald Safer, a former federal prosecutor. In 2012 a post-conviction motion was filed to dismiss the indictment. The motion was dismissed, but in 2014 the Illinois Court of Appeals reversed the dismissal and demanded an evidentiary hearing. Susan Carlson did not live long enough to hear that good news; in 2013 she died of an asthma attack at age sixty-three.

At the hearing, Cook County Circuit Judge Alfredo Maldonado granted Bolden a new trial, citing errors by the police and the credible testimony of the new witnesses. Prosecutors originally planned to retry him and Bolden remained in jail on a one million dollar bail. Unexpectedly, in April of 2016 the prosecutors reversed their course and dropped all formal charges. On April 19, 2016, Bolden walked out of prison as a free man after serving twenty-two years for a crime he didn't commit.

Five days later he saw his son, Dominique, graduate from Goshen College in Goshen, Indiana. Dominique was less than a year old when his father went to prison. Bolden never saw Dominique take his first step. Bolden never saw him run up and down the basketball court as a standout on his college basketball team. But now Bolden saw Dominique walk across the stage and receive his degree in physical education.

Susan Carlson would have been proud.

During his long stint in prison, Bolden had to battle constant despair. In a *Chicago Tribune* article, he said, "For a long time nobody cared. Nobody in the court cared, the appellate courts didn't care, the attorneys my family hired didn't care."[11]

But Susan Carlson cared. David Carlson, Susan's son, shared the joyous moment with the Bolden family. He said his mother would be asking, "What can we do for people who are the next Eddie Bolden?"[12]

That's a fair question for each of us. Susan Carlson was a mother skilled at photography. We don't need a law degree to invest time for the sake of the innocent. The only requirement is an abiding passion for justice, which isn't optional for followers of Jesus.

If we do justice in the public arena—if we advocate for judicial reform and if we advocate for the innocent—I believe the God of justice will use us to correct some of the injustice in this world. Then perhaps—*just perhaps*—more Eddie Boldens will see their sons and daughters grow, mature, and succeed in life.

CHAPTER 10

DOING JUSTICE IN THE PERSONAL ARENA

Ken Sauder's day job is raising grain for the kitchens of America. His agribusiness in southern Illinois is large, time-consuming, and challenging. Like others in the breadbasket of this country, he can talk intelligently about agronomy, machinery, meteorology, or the commodities market.

Despite the considerable demands of his farming enterprise, Ken and his wife, Linda, have invested significant time in the federal and state prisons nearby for more than thirty years. Ken first stepped into the maximum-security Illinois prison in Pontiac as a wide-eyed volunteer in his early twenties. There he met a man who had not received a visit from his family in seventeen years. That experience marked Ken deeply. He woke up the next night with a burden to befriend and minister to prison inmates. For the last three decades he has made regular treks to the prisons, holding Bible studies, leading retreats, giving talks, sharing the gospel, and seeing lives changed.

Archie (not his real name) experienced radical life transformation as an inmate at the Illinois River Correctional Center in Canton, Illinois. Archie was serving a thirty-year sentence for the crimes he committed as a leader in a gang. He came to a weekend

Once born-again, Archie soon realized that he had a difficult and dangerous task—he had to get out of the gang.

meeting Ken led at the prison, heard the gospel, and marvelously came to faith in Christ. Once born-again, Archie soon realized that he had a difficult and dangerous task—he had to get out of the gang. Joining a gang comes at a price. Exiting costs even more. Archie willingly shouldered the abuse and threats received for deserting his "brothers." But exiting came with a reward. Witnessing Archie's life change, four of his other gang leaders in prison also put their trust in Christ.

Archie was recently released from the downstate prison as a 71-year-old man. He's adjusting to life outside its walls and getting reacquainted with his family. It's a challenge, but he has faced bigger hurdles. Freedom also comes with new privileges: he held his new granddaughter for the first time.

WHAT CAN WE DO?

You can be a Ken. In the resources section at the back of this book is a list of organizations deeply involved in legal justice issues in this country and around the world. By visiting their websites you can easily explore numerous ways to personally invest your energies on behalf of the incarcerated. Let's explore some of those ways here.

Minister inside prison walls.

Many highly effective organizations serve the incarcerated. With the rapidly growing prison population, they are constantly in need of more volunteers—like Ken and Linda Sauder—to minister to inmates. The following ways to help are just a starting point.

Lead a Bible study. A seminary degree is not required. If you can guide a small group Bible study at your church, you can do the same with inmates. Some of them may come to faith in Jesus Christ, and others can learn how to reflect the light of Christ in a dark, depressing environment.

Mentor in life skills. Inmates anticipating release from prison often need training in basic life skills they did not receive while growing up. You can help them learn how to job hunt, find suitable housing, be a productive employee, and maintain healthy relationships.

Teach a parenting class. Prisoners are separated from their families, but they remain parents to their children. You can equip them to become better fathers and mothers. Simple parenting lessons drawn from God's Word enable incarcerated parents to show love and support to their children despite their physical absence in the home.

Volunteer outside prison walls.

A person's incarceration affects their family like the aftermath of an exploded bomb: everyone is injured by the shrapnel. Remaining parents are left to manage life with children all alone. On top of this, they bear the social stigma of having a spouse in prison. Finances become messy; relationships become awkward. Needs are ignored—as if the suffering of the family is part of the punishment

> **Remaining parents are left to manage life with children all alone. On top of this, they bear the social stigma of having a spouse in prison.**

deserved by the prisoner. But you can step into the void in simple yet life-changing ways.

Help with the Angel Tree program. One in every twenty-eight children has a parent in prison.[1] A ministry of Prison Fellowship, the Angel Tree program seeks to show Jesus' love to the children of those incarcerated by bringing Christmas gifts and the gospel to their homes. If your church does not participate in the Angel Tree program, contact Prison Fellowship to find one in your area. Buy the gifts and—more importantly—deliver them. Children of inmates often feel abandoned and forgotten. You can bring joy and light to a needy home and children who are loved by Jesus.

Help with the reentry of paroled inmates. Released prisoners face immediate, enormous challenges. The obstacles loom so large that 70 percent are arrested again within two years of their release. They often lack a place to live, clothes to wear, and food to eat. They inevitably need a job, friends, financial help, and a support network. Many organizations, including several in the resources section, can equip and inform you in serving released prisoners. You can help provide the bridge to a released prisoner's successful reentry. You can:

1. Connect them to transitional housing.
2. Provide job contacts.
3. Link them to a good church.
4. Encourage, mentor, and support them in their journey outside the prison walls.

Mobilize your church. There is more than any one of us can do, but thankfully God has provided the church. A local assembly can provide the community, training, and support that a released prisoner desperately needs. Encourage your church leadership to consider a prison ministry as part of its gospel mandate. Take a leadership role in the ministry. Most evangelical churches ignore ministry to the formerly incarcerated, but you can draw attention to this neglected need.

DONATE TOWARD GOOD LEGAL HELP FOR THE POOR

The caseloads of public defenders resemble the plight of the Hebrews in Egypt—they are expected to make more bricks with fewer and fewer resources. By law, everyone in our country who is charged with a crime has the right to an attorney. But the current system is a train wreck. Private attorneys, who possess both the skills and resources to capably defend a case, require sizeable retainers and high hourly fees. Securing their services remains far outside the financial ability of most lower-income people. Lacking other viable options, the defense of the poor is left with the public defender's office, which is notoriously overworked and underfunded.

Without the time or the resources to dedicate to a case, the public defender is unable to provide the legal assistance enjoyed by wealthier clients with private attorneys. The results are predictable. To manage through the overwhelming load, the vast majority of cases involve not a thorough preparation and trial but a plea bargain. One law review journal said, "Public defenders are the only representation to which many of the poor, who are disproportionately members of communities of color, will have access. If public defender services are inadequate, the accused poor will likely be deprived of constitutional procedural protections."[2]

Donating funds to legal aid societies can help ensure that all—regardless of race or income bracket—can receive adequate legal help.

PRAY FOR JUSTICE

Praying is last but not least. In fact, it represents the best we can do. We can unleash the unlimited resources of our God for justice in this country if we plead for His help and enablement. The needs far outstrip the available resources, but Jesus tells us, "Ask, and it will be given to you; seek, and you will find; knock, and it will be opened to you. For everyone who asks receives, and the one who seeks finds, and to the one who knocks it will be opened" (Luke 11:9–10).

The three commands in that passage are in the present tense, indicating that *these are actions we are to continue to do over and over.* We are to continue to ask; we are to constantly seek; we are to unceasingly knock. We are to pray and keep on praying. If we do, Jesus promises that—in the right time and the right way—our loving heavenly Father will respond.

Pray for justice. Here are specific needs to get you started:

1. Pray for the protection of our law enforcement officers in our streets.
2. Pray for wisdom and courage of lawmakers as they consider justice reform.
3. Pray for resources for poorer defendants to secure competent legal help.
4. Pray for discernment of judges and juries as they render verdicts.
5. Pray for the encouragement of inmates as they seek meaning in life behind bars.
6. Pray for provision for families of the incarcerated as they cope with the separation.
7. Pray for justice to roll in our land.

PART 4

WILL WE EVER SEE JUSTICE?

CHAPTER 11

THE REIGN
OF THE JUST KING

W hen I was a pastor, I would occasionally counsel with aged saints who didn't want to be here anymore. They wanted to be in heaven.

Their spouses were in heaven.

Their parents were in heaven.

Their best friends were in heaven.

Their aunts and uncles were in heaven.

Best of all, Jesus was in heaven.

But they were still here on earth. Age had reduced their once-healthy bodies to pain-filled shells of the past. Loneliness gripped their daily experience as they trudged on without the laughter and encouragement of their closest companions. Reflecting on what was in store for them in the "mansion" Jesus had prepared made their wait harder. Every day their yearning for heaven increased. Like Paul, they wanted to "be away from the body and at home with the Lord" (2 Cor. 5:8).

I suspect our discussion on justice has likewise deepened your yearning—not for heaven per se, but for what is right.

You know justice is elusive because we make unjust laws and

have limited knowledge, darkened understanding, and implicit bias.

You are aware that even with the best of intentions, the most dedicated of law-enforcement officers, and the fairest of judges, we will still get it wrong. Many times.

You are not ignorant of the many men and women serving long sentences or even facing the death penalty for crimes they didn't commit. And no one seems to care.

You know that our jails and prisons are populated with an outrageous percentage of minorities, especially African Americans. And it doesn't bother us.

And you yearn for a time when true justice will rule. A day when everything will be made right. This is a good thing. It's a spark placed within us by the Holy Spirit.

The Bible has great news for us: that day is coming! It's not here yet, but God has made us a promise. One day His Son is going to return to this scarred planet in all His power and glory. When He does, He'll establish His prophesied kingdom and rule from His throne in Jerusalem. Justice will no longer be elusive; it will be a reality.

I want to encourage you with this precious truth. Walk with me through the pages of Scripture, and let's see how God's servants describe this righteous reign of Christ.

THE JUST REIGN AS PICTURED BY ISAIAH

Isaiah is often called the Messianic prophet because his sixty-six chapters are laden with predictions of the first and second comings of Christ. At Christmas we recite passages from Isaiah referring to Christ's first advent, such as, "There shall come forth a shoot from the stump of Jesse, and a branch from his roots shall bear fruit. And the Spirit of the LORD shall rest upon him, the Spirit of wisdom and understanding, the Spirit of counsel and might, the Spirit of knowledge and the fear of the LORD" (11:1–2).

We also remember the gripping picture Isaiah presented of Christ's passion and death. In the days leading up to Easter we remind ourselves of the words of Isaiah 53: "He was despised and rejected by men; a man of sorrows and acquainted with grief. . . . Surely he has borne our griefs and carried our sorrows; yet we esteemed him stricken, smitten by God, and afflicted. But he was pierced for our transgressions; he was crushed for our iniquities; upon him was the chastisement that brought us peace, and with his wounds we are healed" (vv. 3–5).

True to form, Isaiah also writes repeatedly of the future day when Christ rules over an earthly kingdom. Such pictures are threaded like a string of diamonds throughout the book, from beginning to end. Let me take you to a handful of those images, especially those that trumpet the justice of His reign.

All peoples will have access to justice (Isaiah 2:1–4).

In chapter 2, Isaiah begins his first major discourse. He immediately signals that he is pointing to a future time called "the latter days," which in this context refer to the millennial reign of Christ. "It shall come to pass *in the latter days* that the mountain of the house of the LORD shall be established as the highest of the mountains, and shall be lifted up above the hills; and all the nations shall flow to it" (v. 2). The "mountain of the house of the LORD" refers to Jerusalem, often called "Mount Zion." Apparently the geography of the land will be altered during Christ's reign, and Jerusalem will enjoy a perch higher than others. The nations of the world will stream to this exalted city, as the center of government.

People will come to Jerusalem with a purpose. "Many peoples shall come and say, 'Come, let us go up to the mountain of the LORD, to the house of the God of Jacob, that he may teach us his ways and that we may walk in his paths'" (v. 3a). Christ will personally be reigning, but people will still be learning the ways of righteousness. Imagine sitting in a class such as Righteousness 101 taught by Jesus! People will still be hampered by a sin nature, but they will have access to God Himself for direction and guidance.

From His throne in Jerusalem, Jesus will dispense justice. "For out of Zion shall go forth the law, and the word of the LORD from Jerusalem. He shall judge between the nations, and shall decide disputes for many peoples" (vv. 3b–4a). When He entered our world in Bethlehem, Jesus came as a humble servant to save us. When He returns to Jerusalem at His second coming, Jesus will come as the majestic King to judge us. Because of sin, disputes between nations will still exist. But Jesus himself will settle the disputes. True justice will prevail and peace will reign as Isaiah predicts, "They shall beat their swords into plowshares, and their spears into pruning hooks; nation shall not lift up sword against nation, neither shall they learn war anymore" (v. 4b).

Justice will come from the seat of authority (Isaiah 9:6–7).

This is another familiar Christmas passage. Isaiah writes these treasured words: "For to us a child is born, to us a son is given; and the government shall be upon his shoulder, and his name shall be called Wonderful Counselor, Mighty God, Everlasting Father, Prince of Peace" (v. 6).

Yet notice that not everything in Isaiah's prophecy was fulfilled in Christ's first coming. A child was born and a son was given, but the government was not "upon his shoulder." The Romans ruled with an iron fist. Therefore, this and other portions of the text await fulfillment upon Christ's return. "Of the increase of his government and of peace there will be no end, on the throne of David and over his kingdom, to establish it and to uphold it *with justice and with righteousness* from this time forth and forevermore.

Jesus will reign on the throne of David, and His kingdom will be characterized by justice and righteousness. Not elusive justice like today, but true justice. It will commence when Christ returns, and it will continue forever as His earthly kingdom gives way to an eternal kingdom.[1] While that may seem impossible to us as we limp in a sin-ravaged world, Isaiah explains, "the zeal of the LORD of the hosts will do this." God's sovereign power will make this happen.

Justice will be dispensed with full knowledge (Isaiah 11:1–5).

I noted earlier how the first two verses of this passage are often associated with Christ's first coming. The remainder of the passage describes the just rule of Christ when He returns. Isaiah writes in verse 3, "And his delight shall be in the fear of the LORD. He shall not judge by what his eyes see, or decide disputes by what his ears hear."

Human judges must rely on the information received through our five senses. Evidence is evaluated and decisions are made by what we see and hear. Unfortunately, we have incomplete knowledge and darkened understanding. We make decisions that are not right or just.

Jesus isn't limited like us. As omniscient God, He knows all things—including the deception hidden in the human heart. Having such comprehensive insight, He will rule justly in all matters. Specifically, Isaiah says, "But with righteousness he shall judge the poor, and decide with equity for the meek of the earth;

and he shall strike the earth with the rod of his mouth, and with the breath of his lips he shall kill the wicked" (v. 4).

Scripture repeatedly tells us that the poor and the vulnerable are to be protected by the king, as they lack resources to protect themselves. Often that doesn't happen. Often two systems of justice exist—one for the powerful and one for the powerless.

Often two systems of justice exist— one for the powerful and one for the powerless.

But when the Just King rules, partiality will be eliminated. The poor will experience "righteousness" and the meek shall know "equity."

Isaiah concludes this picture of Christ's reign in verse 5 when he says, "Righteousness shall be the belt of his waist, and faithfulness the belt of his loins." The belt in biblical times was used to cinch up your robe or tunic so that you could engage in more strenuous activity. Soldiers or workers would gird up their loose robes to keep them from being a hindrance. Using this imagery, Isaiah explains that righteousness (justice) and faithfulness will bind together the reign of the Messiah in His kingdom. Justice will not be elusive. It will be consistently enforced by the righteous King.

Even enemies will receive justice (Isaiah 16:4–5).

This fascinating passage reveals how even the enemies of Judah will gain just treatment from the Messiah. The broader context, beginning in chapter 15, talks about the plight of the Moabites, a downtrodden nation to the east of the Jordan River. In sympathy for them, Isaiah first calls for Judah to provide refuge for the people of Moab from the mighty Assyrian army: "Let the outcasts of Moab sojourn among you; be a shelter to them from the destroyer. When the oppressor is no more, and destruction has ceased, and he who tramples underfoot has vanished from the land . . ." (v. 4).

The historical call from the prophet is to display compassion for the Moabite refugees. Typical of Isaiah's style, this immediately moves to a prophetic picture in the next verse: "Then a throne will be established in steadfast love, and on it will sit in faithfulness in the tent of David one who judges and *seeks justice* and is swift to *do righteousness*" (v. 5).

The Davidic throne belongs to Christ. When He returns to earth, He will sit on it and do justice on the earth. All peoples will experience His justice and righteousness—including outcasts such as the Moabites.

Christ will dispense a gentle justice (Isaiah 42:1–4).

In a cherished part of his prophecy, Isaiah gives us four "servant songs" picturing the Messiah. This is the first, and it is foundational to the other three.[2] Representing the voice of God, Isaiah says of the Coming One, "Behold my servant, whom I uphold, my chosen, in whom my soul delights; I have put my Spirit upon him" (v. 1a).

As God's chosen, Spirit-led leader, Christ will have a justice mission when He returns to earth. Isaiah emphasizes this by repeating it three times within just four verses.

- "He will *bring forth justice* to the nations" (v. 1b)
- "He will faithfully *bring forth justice*" (v. 3)
- "He will not grow faint or be discouraged till he has *established justice* in the earth" (v. 4)

When the just King returns, God's desire for true justice to rule in this world will be realized. Righteousness, justice, and peace will prevail because God's chosen Servant will be ruling. While consistent and comprehensive, this just reign will not be harsh. In the middle of this passage, Isaiah says, "He will not cry aloud or lift up his voice, or make it heard in the street; a bruised reed he will not break, and a faintly burning wick he will not quench" (v. 2–3a).

Christ will be gentle to the oppressed, who are like "bruised reeds" requiring tender care, not jarring discipline. The oppressed are like "faintly burning wicks," which can be extinguished if handled too roughly.

> **Christ will be gentle to the oppressed, who are like "bruised reeds" requiring tender care, not jarring discipline.**

Executing true justice on an earth populated by sin-saturated people may seem a herculean task. Yet Isaiah predicts that the Messiah will be successful in accomplishing his mission. "He *will not grow faint or be discouraged* till he has established justice in the earth" (v. 4).

We can be encouraged because the just King won't be discouraged, and one day—when Christ reigns on this earth—there will be justice in this world.

THE JUST REIGN AS PICTURED IN THE PSALMS

The psalms often depict this perfect rule. Psalms are hymns and worship songs displaying theological truth in poetic language. While many of the psalms speak of the future reign of the Messiah, two emphasize the justice He will bring.

There will be justice for the oppressed (Psalm 72).

This was sung at the coronations of the kings of Israel. It is ascribed to Solomon and may have been a song he wrote either as he ascended the throne of David, or for one of his sons. The psalm affirms the God-empowered role of the king in bringing justice to the people, which was never perfectly executed by human rulers but ultimately points ahead to a Davidic ruler who will be just.

With fanfare, the psalm begins, "Give the king your justice, O God, and your righteousness to the royal son! May he judge your people with righteousness, and your poor with justice!" (vv. 1–2). You can hear the cry of the people in those words. They long for justice to reign. They yearn for righteousness to rule in the land—not the oppression and injustice so typically experienced. Note the group specifically identified, *the poor*. Without resources and often downtrodden, they needed the protection of the king. The psalm enhances this picture in two places. First, in verse 4 it reads, "May he defend the cause of the poor of the people, give deliverance to the children of the needy, and crush the oppressor!"

Don't overlook the key responsibility in the kingly job description. The king is to bring justice to the land, especially for the poor. He is to defend them, deliver them, and fight for them (cf. Prov. 31:4, 8–9).

This emphasis is again seen in verses 12–14: "For he delivers the needy when he calls, the poor and him who has no helper. He has pity on the weak and the needy, and saves the lives of the needy. From oppression and violence he redeems their life, and precious is their blood in his sight." The king accepts this charge as he ascends the throne. He is to hear the cry of the poor, have pity on them, and deliver them from oppression and mistreatment. He is to do so because he places great value on their lives and does not view them as expendable.

The parade of earthly kings who held the throne of David never fulfilled this solemn charge. They couldn't because they were plagued by the same sin nature as the rest of humanity. But a future king will perfectly carry out this divine mandate—Jesus, when He returns in power and glory. One commentator agrees as he writes these words about Psalm 72, "As a royal psalm it prayed for the reigning king, and was a strong reminder of his high calling; yet it exalted this so far beyond the humanly attainable . . . as to suggest for its fulfillment no less a person than the Messiah."[3]

Even the earth itself will rejoice when justice reigns (Psalm 96).

This joyous psalm pictures a millennial scene and should be read in tandem with the words of Paul in Romans 8:19. The apostle, foreseeing the future redemption of the cursed world after Christ's return to earth, says, "For the creation waits with eager longing for the revealing of the sons of God." This psalm paints the same happy picture. Imagine the earth animated with joy: "Let the heavens be glad, and let the earth rejoice; let the sea roar, and all that fills it; let the field exult, and everything in it! Then shall all the trees of the forest sing for joy before the LORD, for he comes (11–13a)."

A choir of cypress trees singing for joy at their redemption. Rocks and rock badgers joining the chorus. The slaps of the ocean on the seashore adding to the praise like well-rehearsed percussion. The entire earth erupting in worship as the chains of its sin-induced curse are finally torn away.

Why all the praise? The Lord has come. And when He comes, He *brings justice to the world*. "Say among the nations, 'The LORD reigns! Yes, the world is established; it shall never be moved; he will judge the peoples with equity'" (v. 10). In the last verse of the psalm, this theme is repeated, "For he comes to judge the earth.

He will judge the world in righteousness, and all the peoples in his faithfulness" (v. 13).

This day is coming. A day when man will no longer pass laws that scream defiance to God's righteous standards. A day when our current corruption will be overwhelmed by a godly government. A day when the most vulnerable of society, like fragile reeds, will stand protected in the loving care of the King. A day when partiality to the powerful will be replaced by the plumb line of God's impartiality. A day when injustice will fade into the mist of the past and justice and righteousness will always prevail.

This day is coming. Jesus is coming back to this earth, as He promised. When He does, justice will no longer be elusive. We will no longer be claiming hollow victories when we get our decisions right and sulking in shame when we don't. The long-awaited King will be enthroned in Jerusalem and all will be right. For as Jesus said, "I judge, and my judgment is just" (John 5:30).

As those who yearn for justice, we cry, "Come quickly, Lord Jesus!"

CHAPTER 12

THE VERDICT OF
THE RIGHTEOUS JUDGE

It's a large headstone for such a small boy. The grave marker at Ivy Hill Cemetery in Cedarbrook, Philadelphia, doesn't bear a name. It simply reads, "America's Unknown Child." Buried in the donated plot are the remains of a boy who had an estimated age of four to six years.

The naked, battered body was discovered February of 1957 by a man checking his muskrat traps in the woods in Fox Chase, Philadelphia. The boy was wrapped in a plaid blanket inside a cardboard box that had once contained a J. C. Penney bassinet. Authorities were initially optimistic that they would quickly identify the boy and nab his killer.

In sixty years, neither has happened.

The child, who obviously met a violent death, is not called by his name and instead is referred to as "the boy in the box." His blonde hair had been cut crudely and close to the scalp. And the one responsible for his death has never been apprehended, despite numerous theories and tips. Even DNA testing and extensive forensic evidence has surfaced no plausible leads. Sadly, it remains the coldest of cold cases.[1]

Many crimes never get solved. Murders, assaults, robberies, and rapes occur daily. Because of the mountain of crimes being investigated by law enforcement officials across the country, many never find resolution. It seems like many perpetrators will escape justice.

But they won't. Perhaps they elude justice in this life. But they cannot escape a final justice.

One day, each and every person will be judged by God. The living and the dead, believers and unbelievers, every person—billions of them—will stand before God in judgment. This is the final justice.

But the nature of the judgment will be different for those who have put their faith in Jesus versus those who haven't. The saved will be judged by Christ to determine the extent of their rewards in eternity. The unsaved will be judged to determine the severity of their punishment in hell.

THE JUDGMENT OF BELIEVERS

An often-overlooked biblical teaching is that believers will be judged by Christ. This doctrine is often neglected because of the wonderful truth that Jesus paid for our sins through His atoning work on the cross. We deserve death because of our sin, but Jesus took our place as the innocent Lamb of God. As a result, when we put our trust in Him we can joyfully claim the words of the apostle Paul in Romans 8:1: "There is therefore now no condemnation for those who are in Christ Jesus."

The doctrine of our future judgment does not negate that central truth; it complements it. We no longer face judgment for our sins. Our eternal destiny has been sealed. We will be in heaven—that's not in question. But as believers, at the time of our death or when we are translated at the rapture, our faithfulness to Christ in this life will be evaluated. This happens at the judgment seat of Christ.

Paul talked about this judgment seat in his two letters to the church in Corinth. In 2 Corinthians 5:10 he wrote, "For we must all appear before the judgment seat of Christ, so that each one may receive what is due for what he has done in the body, whether good or evil." When Paul speaks of this judgment seat, he uses a word that refers to an elevated stand where a judge or ruler would pass judgment on a person. The Corinthians were well acquainted with a judgment seat because they had one in Corinth. It remains in the ruins of that city even today. In Acts 18:12, Paul stood before the judgment seat of Gallio when he was in Corinth.

What will this judgment be like? Paul gives us five characteristics:

It is mandatory.

Paul says, "We *must all* appear." The language indicates it is necessary. It is required. We cannot avoid our day before the judge like we can in our modern court system if we offer a plea bargain. Every believer will one day stand before his Redeemer and face intense scrutiny.

It is individual.

Paul says that the purpose of the judgment is so *"each one* may receive what is due." In a related passage, he confirms that when he says, *"we will all stand* before the judgment seat of God," and *"each* of us will give an account of himself to God" (Rom. 14:10, 12).

When I stand before Christ, the judgment will be about me and only me. When you stand before the judgment seat, it will be about you and only you. It will not be about your parents, your siblings, your best friends, or even your pastors. I will stand alone. You will stand alone. The judgment will be individual.

It will expose everything.

Paul says the judgment will expose "what [each] has done in the body, whether good or evil" (2 Cor. 5:10). Like a divine searchlight, God will bring everything hidden to light. The acts we are proud of and the things we are ashamed of. The moments when we were godly and the times we acted ungodly. God's eyes will see and judge everything.

> **Like a divine searchlight, God will bring everything hidden to light.**

He will expose our deeds. The actions we take, and everything we do. Christ will evaluate whether they are "good or evil."

He will expose our thoughts. While unspoken, Christ will judge the value of our thoughts. In Luke 12:2–3, Christ says, "Nothing is covered up that will not be revealed, or hidden that will not be known. Therefore whatever you have said in the dark shall be heard in the light, and what you have whispered in private rooms shall be proclaimed on the housetops."

He will expose our words. Every word we've ever spoken— even the ones we wish we hadn't—will be judged by Christ at the judgment seat. Jesus said in Matthew 12:36–37, "I tell you, on the day of judgment people will give account for every careless word they speak, for by your words you will be justified, and by your words you will be condemned."

He will expose our motives. We can easily deceive people as to our true motives. Christ will know the real reasons for why we did, said, and thought what we did. In Hebrews 4:12–13 it says that the Word of God is able to discern "the thoughts and intentions of the heart. And no creature is hidden from his sight, but all are naked and exposed to the eyes of him to whom we must give account." *Everything will be exposed.* Not only will we be standing alone before the judgment seat but also every thought, word, deed, and motive will be laid bare before his searching eyes.

It will reveal the eternal value of our work.

Paul says we will receive what we are due, "whether good or evil" (2 Cor. 5:10). The word *evil* is a word that can also be translated as "worthless." It indicates that the judgment seat will reveal if the sum total of our life's work for Christ is valuable to Him or worthless.

In 1 Corinthians 3, Paul explains the process for how the value will be determined by Christ. "Now if anyone builds on the foundation with gold, silver, precious stones, wood, hay, straw—each one's work will become manifest, for the Day will disclose it, because it will be revealed by fire, and the fire will test what sort of work each one has done. If the work that anyone has built on the foundation survives, he will receive a reward. If anyone's work is burned up, he will suffer loss, though he himself will be saved, but only as through fire" (vv. 12–15).

Our works will be tested by fire. Imagine our life's works heaped into a pile, like a mountain of wood for a bonfire—and then torched. The worthless garbage will be consumed; only what withstands the heat of the fire—like precious stones—will remain. In a fleeting moment we will be confronted with the eternal value of our lives. Some, as Paul reveals, will have nothing left. Saved by grace, but void of anything that reveals faithfulness to Christ. Such people will still enjoy heaven, but it will be a deeply embarrassing moment. Paul says, "If anyone's work is burned up, he will suffer loss, though he himself will be saved." Others will see some of their valuable works for Christ remain.

While both fearful and sobering, the test of fire is not so Christ can clearly judge the value of our works. He already knows—He's omniscient. The test of fire is not for His sake—it's for our sake. Our works are subjected to fire before our eyes so *we will know* if our life has had value to Christ. We can be deceived about this. Our desperately wicked hearts can cause us to think certain actions have been valuable to God, when they haven't. In an instant, the truth will be revealed. We will know what moments pleased our Savior—and what time we wasted.

It will lead to rewards—or the loss of them.

Paul says in 1 Corinthians 3:14, "If the work that anyone has built on the foundation survives, he will receive a reward." Jesus reinforces this truth in one of the final verses of the Bible. He says, "Behold, I am coming soon, bringing my recompense with me, to repay everyone for what he has done" (Rev. 22:12).

The recompense Jesus brings is not heaven. For eternal life with Christ in Paradise is not something we earn. Heaven is a free gift given to everyone who believes. Paul shows the folly of trying to earn salvation in Ephesians 2:8–9 when he says, "For by grace you have been saved through faith. And this is not your own doing; it is the gift of God, not a result of works, so that no one may boast."

The recompense Jesus brings is eternal reward. He will evaluate the work of each one of us and determine if we have earned His rewards or forfeited them. The Bible speaks often about such rewards.[2] The rewards vary—from crowns to places of authority in Christ's earthly kingdom. Yet, the greatest reward will be to hear His words of approval—to hear our precious Master say, "Well done!" Imagine the joy of looking into His eyes, seeing a smile on His face, and hearing the words, "I am so pleased with you! I am so delighted with how you served me! Well done! Well done! You are now going to reign with me in my kingdom!"

This is the judgment of believers. It's the judgment seat of Christ. We will all appear. Our life's work will be evaluated as to its value to Christ. Judgment will happen and rewards will be dispensed—or withheld. The results will echo through the rest of eternity.

THE JUDGMENT OF UNBELIEVERS

Final justice also awaits the unsaved. The purpose of this judgment is not to determine the degrees of reward in heaven, but the degrees of punishment in hell. This is a future event often called the great white throne judgment. In the book of Revelation, the apostle John describes the climactic scene like this:

> Then I saw a great white throne and him who was seated on it. From his presence earth and sky fled away, and no place was found for them. And I saw the dead, great and small, standing before the throne, and books were opened. Then another book was opened, which is the book of life. And the dead were judged by what was written in the books, according to what they had done. And the sea gave up the dead who were in it, Death and Hades gave up the dead who were in them, and they were judged, each one of them, according to what they had done. . . . And if anyone's name was not found written in the book of life, he was thrown into the lake of fire. (20:11–13, 15)

In John's sequence, everything tied to the present earth is now gone. The new heaven and the new earth, which will continue for all eternity, have not yet appeared. In the cosmic void that remains, John sees a great throne, signifying grandeur and magnificence. It is also a white throne, displaying its righteousness and holiness. On this great white throne is a great being, for it says, "From his presence earth and sky fled away" (Rev. 20:11).

Who is this judge seated on this majestic, awesome throne? John chooses not to tell us. Revelation gives us hints to the answer. Throughout the book, the Father is always seen as sitting on a throne,[3] and it seems highly probable that He is also on this throne. But it is also possible Christ is sharing the throne with Him. Elsewhere in Revelation this is indeed the case—such as in 3:21 where Jesus says, "The one who conquers, I will grant him to sit with me on my throne, as I also conquered and *sat down with my Father* on his throne." Also, when Jesus was present on earth, He declared all judgment had been given to Him: "The Father judges no one, but has given all judgment to the Son" (John 5:22). This includes the execution of all judgment.[4]

Lacking more clarity from Scripture, I suspect the Father and the Son are sharing this great white throne. I envision the Father possessing the ultimate authority to judge, but entrusting that judging function to the Son as He was the one who gave Himself to redeem man.

Standing before this majestic throne is a vast multitude of resurrected people. They are the unsaved "dead" of all time. From the first unbelievers to die in the early chapters of Genesis, to the last unsaved person to perish during Christ's reign on earth,[5] the coffers of the dead have been emptied—including those who had been lost at sea.[6] Every lost person from every moment in human history is summoned to this roll call. The great and powerful take their place with the weak and lowly. Roman Caesars stand next to slaves. Celebrities share the fearsome moment with street-dwellers. Who you were in life matters not. John Phillips graphically describes the scene like this:

> The dead, small and great, stand before God. Dead souls are united to dead bodies in a fellowship of horror and despair. Little men and paltry women whose lives were filled with pettiness, selfishness, and nasty little sins will be there. Those whose lives amounted to nothing will be here, whose very sins were drab and dowdy, mean, spiteful, peevish, groveling, vulgar, common, and cheap. The great will be there, men who sinned with a high hand, with dash, and courage and flair. Men like Alexander and Napoleon, Hitler and Stalin will be present, men who went in for wickedness on a grand scale with the world for their stage and who died unrepentant at last. Now one and all are arraigned and on their way to be damned: a horrible fellowship congregated together for the first and last time.[7]

This vast crowd—billions of them—will be "standing." This is significant for two reasons. First, it proves they have been resurrected back to life. They are standing, not lying down like the dead. Second, they stand to receive their sentence from the Judge—just like in courtrooms today.

Their sentence is based upon information provided by the books. John tells us that two sets of books are opened. The first set of books provides a record of every man's deeds. God has such a comprehensive ledger. He didn't build it as people lived their lives and history unfolded. As the eternal, omniscient God, He has always known all things actual and all things possible. Every sinful thought, every mean act, every foul word, every hateful betrayal, every harsh remark—everything—has been recorded by God.

This should not surprise us. If mere humans can capture vast oceans of data and effectively mine its depths through powerful, computerized information retrieval systems, it should not startle us that the Creator of the universe has every speck of data on each of His creatures. On that day, God will consult this first set of books. He will know everything.

Then a second book will be opened. The Book of Life.

This is the book of the saved. It contains the list of all whose sins have been forgiven as a result of their faith in Christ. None of those staring at the Judge on that day will have their name recorded in this book. They are all unbelievers.

It should not startle us that the Creator of the universe has every speck of data on each of His creatures.

What happens next can strain our emotions, for we all have relatives, friends, or even immediate family members who land in this category. They lived—and they died—without putting their faith in Christ. While we prayed earnestly, spoke openly, and shared the gospel persistently, they never believed. As a result, we know our loved one will be facing this judgment. And it grieves us.

According to John's writings, the dead were judged by "what was written in the books" (Rev. 20:12). How are these actions weighed? The Bible doesn't say specifically, but there are indications that judgments vary according to the sins committed—just as there are different levels of reward in heaven. Jesus indicated this in Matthew 11 when he condemned the unrepentant cities in Galilee. He said:

Woe to you, Chorazin! Woe to you, Bethsaida! For if the mighty works done in you had been done in Tyre and Sidon, they would have repented long ago in sackcloth and ashes. But I tell you, it will be more bearable on the day of judgment for Tyre and Sidon than for you. And you, Capernaum, will you be exalted to heaven? You will be brought down to Hades. For if the mighty works done in you had been done in Sodom, it would have remained to this day. But I tell you that it will be more tolerable on the day of judgment for the land of Sodom than for you. (vv. 21–24)

This suggests that there are different levels of punishment in hell. For example, let's say Saddam Hussein is brought before the throne. The first book is opened, giving a record of his deeds and graphically confirming that he is a sinner. Every act, word, and thought is listed. Then the second book is opened and bears witness to the fact he is not saved. His name does not appear in the Book of Life.

Everyone—without exception— who stands before the great white throne will be banished to hell because their names are not in the Book of Life. And everyone in hell—without exception— will experience torment. But some will have it worse than others. The deeds of life found in the first book will be consulted. An evil leader who was responsible for the slaughter of millions, such as an Adolf Hitler, will endure more punishment than perhaps a peaceful but unbelieving Aborigine who worked a subsistence farm his entire life. A child rapist and murderer will be sentenced to more torment than a moral, dedicated but unbelieving public school teacher.

Everyone will be judged.

The judgment will be individual.

The judgment will be final.

Most importantly, *the judgment will be right.*

We can and do make mistakes in our rendering of justice today. We lack knowledge, are plagued by sin, and have implicit bias. We do our best, but we make mistakes.

No mistakes will be made on that day. Every judgment will be perfect and right. The omniscient God—who knows everything there is to know and is perfectly just in all his ways—will be pronouncing the sentence.

And finally—*finally!*—true justice will be accomplished.

AFTERWORD

Every day a vast army of dedicated, educated, experienced—yet often unappreciated—people are engaged in our country's criminal justice system. According to the Bureau of Justice, nearly 18,000 law enforcement agencies employ 1.13 million workers, including more than 750,000 sworn officers.[1] Approximately 12,500 judges are distributed between the state and federal systems.[2] More than 1.22 million lawyers practice all manners of law, including many in criminal law.[3] You undoubtedly know a police officer, a judge, or a trial lawyer. You may be one.

The stories in this book may raise questions about the skill or motivation of those involved in law enforcement. *That is not my intent.* I am confident that the overwhelming majority of those wearing the badge, wearing the robe, or defending the accused are committed to seeing justice served. I support and pray for them. The difficulty and complexity of their jobs is almost unrivaled.

I've tried to show that sometimes, despite the diligent efforts of dedicated individuals, we get it wrong. The innocent are convicted, the guilty escape punishment, and justice is not served. Instead, it is maddeningly elusive.

We long for a perfect system. We yearn for a time when true justice will always prevail. But our legal system will always suffer the drag of the sinful human condition. Sin permeates our lives, blurs our thinking, and scars our judgments. Therefore, we will still make mistakes—even horrific ones. As believers who intimately know how the sin nature plagues, we need to expect mistakes.

But at times we do get it right. And such moments can encourage us not to grow weary in the pursuit of what is just and right.

It was the second time David Potchen had robbed a bank, and the second time he did it to get caught. The first time was in 2001. After losing his job as a welder—and subsequently losing his home and truck—he walked into a bank in Hammond, Indiana, with a shotgun and no intention of hurting anyone. He told the bank staff, "Nothing's going to happen. This is just something I had to do because I'm losing everything." He held the staff hostage until the police arrived and arrested him. For his actions he gained nine felony convictions and a thirty-year prison sentence.

When released on parole, Potchen found an $11-an-hour job as a welder and walked miles every day to work from his motel room in Gary, Indiana. He was hard-working, loyal, and honest. But in 2014, in an economic downturn, he was laid off from his job. He looked for work with three other companies who were within walking distance of his motel, but because of his criminal record he found nothing.

Eventually he ran out of money and lost his motel room. Potchen hit the road and walked twelve miles to Merrillville. Homeless, hungry, cold, and with sore feet, he spent the night in the woods. That night he decided to rob the town's Chase bank the next day.

On June 5, 2014, Potchen walked into the bank without a weapon and scribbled a note to the bank teller on the back of his last résumé: "Give me all your cash in fives and tens." The teller gave him $1,650, and Potchen stuffed the money in his back pocket, walked outside, and waited. He didn't intend to steal the money. He intended to get back in jail, where he'd have a bed and three meals a day. He said, "Once I ran out of money, I couldn't bear the thought of losing everything again. I went inside, took the money, sat on the curb and waited for [the police] to come."

When Potchen appeared before Lake Superior Court Judge Clarence Murray, he pled guilty and asked for the maximum sentence of eight years. Judge Murray, the son of a minister, discerned that a jail sentence was not the right action. He said in court, "You're not a throwaway, Mr. Potchen. You

"You're not a throwaway, Mr. Potchen."

have value, sir, I'm always optimistic and hopeful that there are still good people out there who believe freedom is important." He didn't slap him in jail. He put him on probation.

A newspaper reporter ran the story and job offers poured in for Potchen. A company in northwest Indiana that makes frames for RVs hired him as a welder. He reports monthly to a probation officer, but staying clean and out of trouble is not a problem for him. He said, "I don't drink. I don't smoke. I don't do anything. . . . All I do is work, work, work." He settled into a one-bedroom apartment and has excelled at his new job. His one hobby is fishing, so he eventually bought a boat.

When Potchen had his last parole hearing before Judge Murray in March of 2016, he said to the judge, "I appreciate what you've all done for me, especially you, Judge Murray. Is there any chance that I could come up there and shake your hand?" Judge Murray smiled and agreed. He approached the bench and the two men shook hands.[4]

This is justice.

We don't always get it right, but let's rejoice when we do.

Let's work diligently and compassionately to correct what we get wrong. And let's never stop yearning for the day when the just King will rule and *all* will be made right.

RESOURCES

Books Through Bars

"A volunteer-run organization that distributes free books and educational materials to incarcerated people." | **booksthroughbars.org**

Christian Legal Society

"Seeking Justice with the Love of God." | **clsnet.org/legalaid**

Families Against Mandatory Minimums

"Fighting for smart sentencing laws that protect public safety." | **famm.org**

Impact Fund

"Public Interest Law Non-Profit Organization." | **impactfund.org**

The Innocence Project

"Litigation and public policy organization dedicated to exonerating wrongfully convicted individuals through DNA testing and reforming the criminal justice system to prevent future injustice." | **innocenceproject.org**

The International Justice Mission

"Rescue thousands, protect millions, prove that justice for the poor is possible." | **ijm.org**

John Jay College of Criminal Justice—Prisoner Reentry Institute (PRI)

"Easing reentry and guiding justice-involved people . . . as they successfully reintegrate into their communities as thriving members of society." | **johnjaypri.org**

Just Detention International

"A health and human rights organization that seeks to end sexual abuse in all forms of detention." | **justdetention.org**

Just Leadership USA

"Dedicated to cutting the US correctional population in half by 2030." | **justleadershipusa.org**

Legal Services for Prisoners with Children

"Organizes communities impacted by the criminal justice system and advocates to release incarcerated people, to restore human and civil rights, and to reunify families and communities." | **prisonerswithchildren.org**

National Criminal Justice Organization

"A national voice in shaping and implementing criminal justice policy." | **www.ncja.org**

National H.I.R.E. Network

Work to "increase the number and quality of job opportunities available to people with criminal records by changing public policies, employment practices, and public opinion." | **hirenetwork.org**

Nation Inside

"A platform that connects and supports people who are building a movement to systematically challenge mass incarceration." | **nationinside.org**

Prison Fellowship

"Prison Fellowship trains and inspires churches and communities—inside and outside of prison—to support the restoration of those affected by incarceration." | **prisonfellowship.org**

RAND Corporation—Prisoner Reentry

"RAND research has explored how to prevent recidivism through correctional education, the public health issues of prisoner reentry, and the question of prisoner rehabilitation." | **rand.org/topics/prisoner-reentry**

Reentry Central

"The national website for news and information on the subject of reentry and related criminal justice issues." | **reentrycentral.org**

Sentencing Project

Working for "a fair and effective U.S. criminal justice system." | **sentencingproject.org**

Vera Institute of Justice

"To urgently build and improve justice systems that ensure fairness, promote safety, and strengthen communities." | **vera.org**

Women and Prison

"Promote strategies and actions that challenge the system and the ways that it reproduces all forms of discrimination, violence, and social injustice in the treatment of women and their families." | **womenandprison.org**

NOTES

Introduction
1. Steve Mills, "Innocent Prisoners Jailed in Same Cell Forge Friendship, and Freedom," *Chicago Tribune*, December 19, 2015, http://www.chicagotribune .com/news/ct-innocent-cellmates-met-1220-20151218-story.html.
2. R. C. Sproul, *One Holy Passion: The Attributes of God* (Nashville: Thomas Nelson, 1987), 110.
3. The best works on social justice include Timothy Keller, *Generous Justice: How God's Grace Makes Us Just* (New York: Penguin, 2010); Nicholas Wolterstorff, *Justice: Rights and Wrongs* (Princeton: Princeton University Press, 2008); Ken Wytsma, *Pursuing Justice: the Call to Live & Die for Bigger Things* (Nashville: Thomas Nelson, 2013); Barry H. Corey, *Love Kindness: Discover the Power of a Forgotten Christian Virtue* (Carol Stream, IL: Tyndale, 2016).

Chapter 1: The Starting Point for Justice
1. "Western Theories of Justice: Immanuel Kant," Internet Encyclopedia of Philosophy, accessed March 19, 2016, http://www.iep.utm.edu/justwest/#SH4a/.
2. John K. Roth, ed. *Ethics*, rev. ed. (Pasadena, CA: Salem Press, 2005), 801.
3. Karen Lebacqz, *Six Theories of Justice: Perspectives from Philosophical and Theological Ethics* (Minneapolis: Augsburg Publishing House, 1986), 30.
4. A. W. Tozer, *The Knowledge of the Holy* (Lincoln, NE: Back to the Bible Broadcast, 1961), 113.
5. R. C. Sproul, *One Holy Passion: The Attributes of God* (Nashville: Thomas Nelson, 1987), 111.

Chapter 3: The Legislative Reason: We Make Unjust Laws
1. Charles J. Ogletree Jr. provides a complete account of this incident in "When Law Fails: History, Genius, and Unhealed Wounds after Tulsa's Race Riot," in *When Law Fails: Making Sense of Miscarriages of Justice*, ed. Charles J. Ogletree Jr. and Austin Sarat (New York: New York University Press, 2009), 50–69.
2. Jim Crow laws refer to the formal, codified system of racial apartheid that dominated the American South for three-quarters of a century, beginning in the 1890s. The name Jim Crow apparently comes from a minstrel act.
3. "Letter from a Birmingham Jail," public domain, accessed August 6, 2016, at University of Pennsylvania's Africa Studies Center, https://www.africa.upenn .edu/Articles_Gen/Letter_Birmingham.html.
4. Chicago Municipal Code, sec. 36034.

5. "Racial Integrity Laws (1924–1930)," Encyclopedia Virginia (website), accessed May 23, 2016, http://www.encyclopediavirginia.org/Racial_Integrity_Laws_of_the_1920s.

6. "A Shameful History: Eugenics in Virginia," ACLU (website), accessed March 30, 2016, https://acluva.org/10898/a-shameful-history-eugenics-in-virginia.

Chapter 4: The Cognitive Reason: We Have Limited Knowledge

1. For a compelling interview of Brown by George M. Anderson, see "Fourteen Years on Death Row: An Interview with Joseph Green Brown," *AMERICA* magazine, March 29, 1997, accessed May 23, 2016, www.deathpenaltyinfo.org/14years.pdf.

2. Mary L. Dudziak, "The Case of 'Death for a Dollar Ninety-Five': Miscarriages of Justice and Constructions of American Identity," in *When Law Fails: Making Sense of Miscarriages of Justice*, ed. Charles J. Ogletree Jr. and Austin Sarat (New York: New York University Press, 2009), 25–48.

3. Ibid., 36.

4. See also "Top Ten Wrongful Convictions Overturned by DNA Evidence," Listland (website), accessed March 19, 2015, http://www.listland.com/top-10-wrongful-convictions-overturned-by-dna-evidence.

5. See "DNA Exonerations in the United States," Innocence Project (website), accessed May 23, 2016, http://www.innocenceproject.org/dna-exonerations-in-the-united-states.

6. Adam Benforado, *Unfair: The New Science of Criminal Injustice* (New York: Crown, 2015), 101.

7. Quoted by Anderson, "Fourteen Years on Death Row," 20.

Chapter 5: The Spiritual Reason: We Have Darkened Understanding

1. Nicholas Wolterstorff, *Justice: Rights and Wrongs* (Princeton: Princeton University Press, 2008), 40.

Chapter 6: The Neurological Reason: We Have Implicit Bias

1. Jon Cohen and Dan Balz, "Race Shapes Zimmerman Verdict Reaction," *Washington Post,* July 22, 2013, https://www.washingtonpost.com/politics/race-shapes-zimmerman-verdict-reaction/2013/07/22/3569662c-f2fc-11e2-8505-bf6f231e77b4_story.html.

2. David Brooks, "Beware Stubby Glasses," *New York Times*, January 10, 2013, http://www.nytimes.com/2013/01/11/opinion/brooks-beware-stubby-glasses.html.

3. "Boston University's 141st Commencement Baccalaureate Address: Nancy Hopkins," Boston University (website), May 18, 2014, http://www.bu.edu/news/2014/05/19/boston-universitys-141st-commencement-baccalaureate-address-nancy-hopkins.

5. Cheryl Staats et al., *State of the Science: Implicit Bias Review 2015,* Kirwan Institute, 22, PDF accessed July 8, 2016, http://kirwaninstitute.osu.edu/researchandstrategicinitiatives/implicit-bias-review.

6. "The Effect of Race and Sex on Physicians' Recommendations for Cardiac Catheterization," *New England Journal of Medicine*, February 25, 1999, accessed May 23, 2016, http://www.nejm.org/doi/full/10.1056/NEJM199902253400806.

7. "Racial Disproportionality in School Discipline: Implicit Bias is Heavily Implicated," Kirwan Institute (blog), February 5, 2016, http://kirwaninstitute.osu.edu/racial-disproportionality-in-school-discipline-implicit-bias-is-heavily-implicated.

8. Ibid.

9. *Housing Discrimination Against Racial and Ethnic Minorities 2012*, PDF accessed April 15, 2016, http://www.huduser.gov/portal/Publications/pdf/HUD-514_HDS2012.pdf.

10. M. W. Anderson and V. C. Plaut, quoted in Cheryl Staats, *State of the Science: Implicit Bias Review 2014*, Kirwan Institute, 59, PDF accessed July 8, 2016, http://kirwaninstitute.osu.edu/researchandstrategicinitiatives/implicit-bias-review.

11. Marianne Bertrand and Sendhil Mullainathan, "Are Emily and Greg More Employable Than Lakisha and Jamal? A Field Experiment on Labor Market Discrimination," *American Economic Review* 94, no. 4 (September 2004): 991–1013.

12. Cheryl Staats et al., *State of the Science: Implicit Bias Review 2015,* Kirwan Institute, 22, PDF accessed July 8, 2016, http://kirwaninstitute.osu.edu/researchandstrategicinitiatives/implicit-bias-review.

13. Adam Benforado, *Unfair: The New Science of Criminal Injustice* (New York: Crown, 2015), xiv.

14. Wesley Lowery, "Study finds police fatally shoot unarmed black men at disproportionate rates," *Washington Post*, April 7, 2016, https://www.washingtonpost.com/national/study-finds-police-fatally-shoot-unarmed-black-men-at-disproportionate-rates/2016/04/06/e494563e-fa74-11e5-80e4-c381214de1a3_story.html.

15. Ibid.

16. Charles Ogletree, Robert J. Smith, and Johanna Wald, "Coloring Punishment: Implicit Social Cognition and Criminal Justice," in *Implicit Racial Bias across the Law*, ed. Justin D. Levinson & Robert J. Smith (New York: Cambridge University Press, 2012), 48.

17. Cheryl Staats and Charles Patton, *State of the Science: Implicit Bias Review 2013,* Kirwan Institute, 39, PDF accessed May 23, 2016, http://kirwaninstitute.osu.edu/researchandstrategicinitiatives/implicit-bias-review.

18. Ibid.

19. Staats et al., *Implicit Bias Review 2015*, 13.

20. Sarah Jane Forman, "The #Ferguson Effect: Opening the Pandora's Box of Implicit Racial Bias in Jury Selection," *Northwestern University Law Review* 109, no. 171 (2005): 171–79.

21. Dallas Franklin, "While 'affluenza' teen went free, similar case led to 20 years in prison," News Channel 4 (website), accessed April 27, 2016, http://kfor.com/2016/02/16/while-affluenza-teen-went-free-similar-case-led-to-20-years-in-prison.

22. The next chapter to this story was recently written when Couch violated parole and left the country. Arrested at a Mexican resort, he returned to face charges in adult court and was sentenced to two years in prison. Nomaan Merchant, "Judge gives Texas 'affluenza' teen nearly 2 years in jail," April 13, 2016, http://bigstory.ap.org/article/66a083aa388c415d87708e6439cff6dd/texas-affluenza-teen-have-first-hearing-adult-court.

23. "Police Accountability Task Force Report" (website), accessed April 27, 2016, https://chicagopatf.org.
24. Ibid.
25. Robert. J. Smith and G. Ben Cohen, "Choosing Life or Death (Implicitly)," in Levinson and Smith, *Implicit Racial Bias across the Law*, 229.
26. Ibid, 230.
27. Ibid.
28. Ibid., 232.
29. Ibid., 237.
30. "Studies: Racial Bias Among Jurors in Death Penalty Cases," Death Penalty Information Center, accessed October 18, 2016, http://www.deathpenalty info.org/studies-racial-bias-among-jurors-death-penalty-cases.
31. Smith and Cohen, "Choosing Life or Death (Implicitly)," 233.
32. Adam Benforado, *Unfair: The New Science of Criminal Injustice* (New York: Crown, 2015), 199.
33. Quoted by Smith and Cohen in "Choosing Life or Death (Implicitly)," 229.
34. To view the instrument, see "Project Implicit," accessed May 23, 2016, https://implicit.harvard.edu/implicit/education.html.
35. Julia Edwards, "Justice Dept. mandates 'implicit bias' training for agents, lawyers," Reuters (website), June 27, 2016, http://www.reuters.com/article/us-usa-justice-bias-exclusive-idUSKCN0ZD251.
36. See the excellent article by Jennifer K. Elek and Paula Hannaford-Agor, "Implicit Bias and the American Juror," *Court Review* 51, 116–21, PDF accessed July 8, 2016, http://www.ncsc-jurystudies.org/~/media/Microsites/Files/CJS/What%20We%20Do/Elek%20%20Hannaford-Agor%22015%20-%20Implicit%20bias%20and%20the%20American%20juror.ashx.

Chapter 8: Doing Justice in the Political Arena

1. "The Constitution of the United States," accessed May 25, 2016, http://constitutionus.com.
2. Term coined by Wayne Grudem, *Politics According to the Bible: A Comprehensive Resource for Understanding Modern Political Issues in Light of Scripture* (Grand Rapids: Zondervan, 2010). This term is a right view of the role Christians must play in the political process.
3. Ibid., 69.
4. Stephen V. Monsma, *Pursuing Justice in a Sinful World* (Grand Rapids: Eerdmans, 1984), 22.
5. Outlined in J. Paul Nyquist, *Prepare: Living Your Faith in an Increasingly Hostile Culture* (Chicago: Moody, 2015), 42–45.
6. "Declaration of Independence," Charters of Freedom (website), accessed May 27, 2016, http://www.archives.gov/exhibits/charters/declaration_transcript .html.
7. "First Amendment to the United States Constitution," Wikipedia, accessed May 27, 2016, https://en.wikipedia.org/wiki/First_Amendment_to_the_United_States_Constitution.
8. Nyquist, *Prepare*, 25–40.
9. The 1997 US Supreme Court decision ruled that the Religious Freedom Restoration Act (RFRA) of 1993 is not applicable to state laws. If a state wishes to defend religious freedoms, it must enact a state law.

10. "Incarceration," The Sentencing Project (website), accessed May 23, 2016, http://www.sentencingproject.org/template/page.cfm?id=107.
11. Douglas A. Berman, "Extreme Punishment," in *When Law Fails: Making Sense of Miscarriages of Justice*, ed. Charles J. Ogletree Jr. and Austin Sarat (New York: New York University Press, 2009), 165.
12. Leith Anderson and Galen Carey, *Faith in the Voting Booth: Practical Wisdom for Voting Well* (Grand Rapids: Zondervan, 2016), 132.
13. Charles Ogletree, Robert J. Smith, and Johanna Wald, "Coloring Punishment," in *Implicit Racial Bias across the Law*, ed. Justin D. Levinson & Robert J. Smith (New York: Cambridge University Press, 2012), 45.
14. Adam Benforado, *Unfair: The New Science of Criminal Injustice* (New York: Crown, 2015), 209.
15. National Association of Evangelicals, *Sentencing Reform 1983*, accessed July 15, 2016, http://nae.net/sentencing-reform.
16. Reid Wilson, "Tough Texas Gets Results by Going Softer on Crime," *Washington Post*, November 27, 2014, https://www.washingtonpost.com/blogs/govbeat/wp/2014/11/27/tough-texas-gets-results-by-going-softer-on-crime.
17. Nicholas Wolterstorff, *Justice: Rights and Wrongs* (Princeton: Princeton University Press, 2008), 75.
18. John D. Sutter, "Silent Crisis: 1 in 5 American kids is poor," CNN.com, September 23, 2014, http://www.cnn.com/2014/09/23/opinion/sutter-child-poverty-casey-foundation.
19. "Child Hunger Facts," Feeding America (website), accessed May 23, 2016, http://www.feedingamerica.org/hunger-in-america/impact-of-hunger/child-hunger/child-hunger-fact-sheet.html.
20. I applaud the efforts of Anderson and Carey in their book *Faith in the Voting Booth* and urge every concerned Christian to study its helpful, practical contents.
21. R. C. Sproul, *One Holy Passion: The Attributes of God* (Nashville: Thomas Nelson, 1987), 117.

Chapter 9: Doing Justice in the Public Arena

1. Jennifer Gonnerman, "Before the Law," *New Yorker*, October 6, 2014, http://www.newyorker.com/magazine/2014/10/06/before-the-law.
2. Ibid.
3. Jennifer Gonnerman, "Kalief Browder, 1993–2015," *New Yorker*, June 7, 2015, http://newyorker.com/news/news-desk/kalief-browder-1993-2015.
4. Richard M. Aborn and Ashley D. Cannon, "Prisons: In Jail But Not Sentenced," *Americas Quarterly* (Winter 2013), accessed July 15, 2016, http://www.americasquarterly.org/aborn-prisons.
5. See Daniel Foster, "The Yellow Menace," *National Review*, June 8, 2011, http://www.nationalreview.com/corner/269986/yellow-menace-daniel-foster. For a review of the lemonade wars, see Erik Kain, "The Inexplicable War on Lemonade Stands," *Forbes*, August 3, 2011, http://www.forbes.com/sites/erikkain/2011/08/03/the-inexplicable-war-on-lemonade-stands/#7c8811 b82264.
6. Matt Hickman, "Gary Harrington, Oregon Resident, Sentenced to Jail for Stockpiling Rainwater," *The Huffington Post*, April 10, 2013, http://www.huffingtonpost.com/2012/08/16/gary-harrington-oregon-water-rainwater_n_1784378.html.

7. For an excellent historical review of the sentencing process, see "Chapter 3: Policies and Practices Contributing to High Rates of Incarceration," in Jeremy Travis, Bruce Western, and Steve Redburn, eds., *The Growth of Incarceration in the United States: Exploring Causes and Consequences* (Washington, D.C.: National Academies Press, 2014), accessed July 5, 2016, http://www.nap.edu/read/18613/chapter/5.

8. Evan Bernick and Paul Larkin, "Reconsidering Mandatory Minimum Sentences: The Arguments for and against Potential Reforms," The Heritage Foundation (website), February 10, 2014, http://www.heritage.org/research/reports/2014/02/reconsidering-mandatory-minimum-sentences-the-arguments-for-and-against-potential-reforms.

9. Chandra Bolzeko, "Why We Let Prison Rape Go On," *New York Times*, April 17, 2015, http://www.nytimes.com/2015/04/18/opinion/why-we-let-prison-rape-go-on.html.

10. "Felony Disenfranchisement," The Sentencing Project (website), accessed July 6, 2016, http://www.sentencingproject.org/issues/felony-disenfranchisement.

11. Steve Schmadeke and Grace Wong, "Eddie Bolden freed: Suburban mom key figure behind release after 2 decades in prison," *Chicago Tribune*, April 20, 2016, http://www.chicagotribune.com/news/local/breaking/ct-charges-dismissed-convicted-murderer-released-met-20160419-story.html.

12. Ibid.

Chapter 10: Doing Justice in the Personal Arena

1. "FAQs About Children of Prisoners," Prison Fellowship (website), accessed July 6, 2016, https://www.prisonfellowship.org/resources/training-resources/family/ministry-basics/faqs-about-children-of-prisoners.

2. Charles J. Ogletree Jr., "An Essay on the New Public Defender for the 21st Century," *Law and Contemporary Problems* 58, no. 1 (1995): 84, PDF accessed July 5, 2016, http://scholarship.law.duke.edu/cgi/viewcontent.cgi?article=4267&context=lcp.

Chapter 11: The Reign of the Just King

1. See Daniel 2 and Revelation 20–21.

2. For the other three servant songs, see Isaiah 49:1–13; 50:4–11; 52:13–53:12.

3. Derek Kidner, *Psalms 1–72* (Downers Grove, IL: InterVarsity Press, 1973), 254.

Chapter 12: The Verdict of the Righteous Judge

1. For a good synopsis of all the leads followed to find the murderer of the "boy in the box," see "The Boy in the Box Mystery," America's Unknown Child (website), accessed May 23, 2016, http://americasunknownchild.net/summary.htm.

2. See Matthew 6, 19, Luke 19, and Hebrews 6 for examples of rewards in the New Testament.

3. For examples, see Revelation 5:13 ("To him who sits on the throne and to the Lamb be blessing and honor and glory and might forever and ever!") and 6:16 ("Fall on us and hide us from the face of him who is seated on the throne, and from the wrath of the Lamb").

4. John 5:27.
5. Revelation 20:7–10 describes the last revolt of Satan and the destruction of his army—which apparently consists of unbelievers who refused to trust in Jesus despite His personal reign on earth.
6. Revelation 20:13.
7. John Phillips, *Exploring Revelation*, rev. ed. (Neptune, NJ: Loizeaux, 1991), 242–43.

Afterword

1. "Local Police," Bureau of Justice Statistics (website), accessed July 1, 2016, http://www.bjs.gov/index.cfm?ty=tp&tid=71.
2. Approximately 9,200 are state judges and 3,300 are federal judges. See "Federal District Judges are Vastly Outnumbered by State Judges," Public Citizen PDF accessed July 1, 2016, https://www.citizenarchive.org/documents/FederalDistricJudgesvastlyoutnumberedbystatejudges.pdf.
3. Jeff Jacoby, "US legal bubble can't pop soon enough," *The Boston Globe*, May 9, 2014, https://www.bostonglobe.com/opinion/2014/05/09/the-lawyer-bubble-pops-not-moment-too-soon/qAYzQ823qpfi4GQl2OiPZM/story.html.
4. Numerous news agencies followed this story in the Chicago area. For key parts of this episode I am indebted to the reporting of John Kass, "Bank robber who just wanted to work gets a second chance," *Chicago Tribune*, March 17, 2016, http://www.chicagotribune.com/news/columnists/kass/ct-bank-robber-second-chance-0318-20160317-column.html; and Ruth-Ann Krause, "A year later, bank robber thanks judge for 2nd chance," *Chicago Tribune*, March 19, 2016, http://www.chicagotribune.com/suburbs/post-tribune/news/ct-ptb-potchen-meets-judge-st-0318-20160317-story.html.

ACKNOWLEDGMENTS

I am not a skilled writer. I am an educational administrator who often struggles to record rambling thoughts on a page. Fortunately, I have been surrounded by a talented ensemble who augment my feeble efforts. I am deeply grateful for the following people who have made this book possible:

Randall Payleitner, Matt Boffey, and the editorial team at Moody Publishers, who enthusiastically supported the project, honed the message, and made the final product better. Thank you for your encouragement!

Ajit Christopher, who interrupted his final semester as a seminary student to provide valuable research for me. Your contributions were numerous and necessary.

Natalie Nyquist, who provided constant counsel and amazing edits throughout the writing process. I am blessed to have a daughter with your skill set by my side!

Steve Mogck, Junias Venugopal, Janet Stiven, Greg Thornton, and Ken Heulitt. On those days when I slipped into my cave to write, you faithfully led the Institute. I am grateful for your skill, dedication, and support.

The Board of Trustees at Moody, who provide me with the freedom to write. Thank you for investing in me and our students. One day you will receive your reward from the Master.

Finally, I give thanks and praise to the Just King, the Lord Jesus Christ. You rule now from heaven. One day you will reign on earth. We patiently wait for the justice and righteousness of your kingdom. "Your Kingdom come, your will be done, on earth as it is in heaven."

THE POST-
CHURCH CHRISTIAN

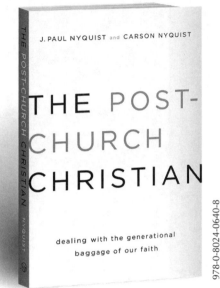

J. PAUL NYQUIST and CARSON NYQUIST

**THE POST-
CHURCH
CHRISTIAN**

dealing with the generational
baggage of our faith

978-0-8024-0640-8

You've heard the stats by now: the Millennial generation is leaving the church.

Walking away in disillusionment and frustration, they are looking for new communities to welcome them. As they seek to follow Jesus, they are leaving the churches they grew up in to find a new way.

What will it look like as the two largest generations today intersect in leadership of the church?

MOODY
Publishers™

From the Word to Life

www.MoodyPublishers.com

From the Word *to Life*

Moody Radio produces and delivers compelling programs filled with biblical insights and creative expressions of faith that help you take the next step in your relationship with Christ.

You can hear Moody Radio on 36 stations and more than 1,500 radio outlets across the U.S. and Canada. Or listen on your smartphone with the Moody Radio app!

www.moodyradio.org